LAND OF THE SPIRIT?
The Australian Religious Experience

LAND OF THE SPIRIT?
The Australian Religious Experience

Muriel Porter

WCC PUBLICATIONS, GENEVA

The Joint Board of Christian Education, Melbourne

Published by WCC Publications, Geneva, in collaboration
with The Joint Board of Christian Education, Melbourne
ISBN 2-8254-0977-4 (WCC)
ISBN 0-85819 800-2 (JBCE)

Cover design: Rob Lucas
Cover photo: Ron Ryan
© 1990 WCC Publications, World Council of Churches,
150 route de Ferney, 1211 Geneva 2, Switzerland
No. 44 in the Risk book series / WCC Publications
Printed in Switzerland

Table of Contents

Preface

Telling the story of Australia's religious experience, past and present, has been challenging. The religious history of Australia has not yet been thoroughly documented, let alone analyzed. There are few comprehensive studies of individual denominations or regions, and while there have been some outstanding biographies, and fine work in some specialist areas, the omissions are enormous. Likewise regular and systematic research on contemporary religious issues is only just beginning to flourish in Australia.

Given a demanding timetable, no original research has been possible. I have had to rely on the work of the few who have travelled this way before. I am conscious there are many gaps that are impossible at present to fill. Reasons of space have also governed selection of material. In a book designed primarily to interest a wide international and local readership, it has also been inappropriate to include much of the small detail that some readers might expect to find here. But the over-riding aim has been to provide a general, rather than comprehensive, picture of the place of religion in Australian life, and to analyze what that means in this particular nation.

Many people have offered their ideas and insights as this book has progressed. I am particularly grateful to my friends and colleagues, the Rev. Prof. Ian Breward, Ms Mavis Grierson, the Rev. Dr David Merritt and Archdeacon Alan Nichols for constructive criticism and evaluation of the text. But though I have relied a great deal on them, and on the secondary sources I have used for my raw materials, ultimately this assessment of Australia's religious experience is mine alone. Not all will agree with it, but hopefully it will stimulate some creative debate in the future.

Introduction

Early in the seventeenth century, a devout Portuguese mariner, Pedro de Quiros, set out to find the mythical southern continent. Europeans had long suspected that such a land existed. Like so many before and after him, de Quiros failed in his mission, but that did not deter him from naming the unknown country "Austrialia del Espiritu Santo" — the south land of the Holy Spirit. De Quiros's romantic quest later caught the imagination of nineteenth-century Roman Catholics in Australia, some of whom believed fervently that de Quiros had indeed succeeded, and that a Roman Catholic had been the true "discoverer" of the world's smallest continent.

Historians today have no doubt that the land de Quiros "discovered" was the New Hebrides. He had not landed on Australia's shores at all. Other explorers did in the years that followed, but the decisive landfall was that of an English Protestant, Captain James Cook.

This outstanding seaman landed at Botany Bay, just south of the present location of Sydney, in April 1770. He then sailed on up the east coast of the vast continent until he reached its northernmost tip. There, he formally took possession of the whole country in the name of King George III of England, calling it "New South Wales". It would not be named Australia until well into the following century.

Cook, respectful of the Australian Aborigines he encountered on his brief visit, nevertheless assumed that their country was free for the taking by the British empire. As a man of his time, it never occurred to him that he was infringing the rights of an ancient people, who did not presume to "own" this land. On the contrary, they — and their descendants today — claimed that the land owned them.

While the great south land may have been an exciting new discovery for Europeans, it was already the home of a civilization far older than anything in their "old" world. And while de Quiros had set out to bring Christianity to the southern continent, he little dreamt that that land was already a sacred place. For the Aborigines held it in trust not as their property, but as the home of their creator.

None of this was known to Cook, or the British government to which he reported. Eighteen years later, anxious to secure this new possession in the face of French ambition, and to create a place to dump their convicts, the British decided to found a colony in New South Wales. So British Australia was born.

Today, Australia is a fully autonomous, independent nation, as it has been since the beginning of this century. But the British flag remains part of Australia's flag, testifying to a heritage that

---

The Creation in Aboriginal Spirituality

In Aboriginal spirituality, the creation of the world began in the Dreaming. Before the Dreaming, there was a pre-existent formless substance, in which spirit beings lived. In some of the stories of the creation event, the Rainbow Serpent emerged from her long sleep underground when she realized her time to give birth had come. She set free the spirit beings to create hills and valleys, light and shade, water, trees and flowers, and all living things. So Australia, in all its distinctive colour and beauty, was born. The Serpent also set free the spirit beings to create the animals and the human beings in a particular relationship with each other, forever related through story, song and ceremony. The snake — called Kabul by some tribes, Borlung or Ngalyod by others, and the Carpet Snake by white people — is regarded as the mother of the earth, the mother of all, and the spirit of the land. She is most closely in touch with humans at special sacred sites, her resting places. All the land, however, is sacred.

---

many Australians still honour. The British sovereign is Queen of Australia. Although the days of the British empire are no more, Australia remains a member of the (British) Commonwealth of Nations. But the "colonial cringe" has only recently vanished from Australian attitudes.

Australia is a thriving nation of 16.25 million people, in a land roughly the size of the United States of America. Much of the vast continent is sparsely populated, however, as 70 percent of Australia's people live in its ten largest cities. All but one of those cities are strung out along the nation's long sea coast, the fertile rim of a generally harsh and forbidding interior. As is to be expected in a country this size, the climate and scenery vary dramatically, from rainforests to snowfields, from barren deserts to lush green plains.

The pattern of its earliest white settlements can be traced in its political boundaries. The six original British colonies are now the six Australian states, retaining considerable autonomy within a federation inaugurated in 1901. Sydney, capital of the first colony, New South Wales, retains its historic precedence, and is the largest city. But it is not the seat of the federal government. Canberra was created earlier this century to avoid the powerful colonial rivalries which bedevilled the relationship between Sydney and Melbourne, the second largest city. Canberra remains, in many respects, an artificial place remote from the lives of ordinary Australians.

In the last decade of the twentieth century, Australia is fast-developing as a fascinating multicultural society with its own distinctive ethos. As an international trading nation, it shares many of the world's economic problems, and few of its citizens would pretend that life here is perfect. Clearly it is not, and too many Australians suffer from the inequities which have seen the rich growing richer as the poor grow poorer. Poverty in Australia, as in other Western countries, too often wears a female face as increasingly large numbers of sole mothers struggle to bring up families. Aborigines still suffer from long years of injustice. But Australia, nevertheless, is a democracy whose people are as free and equal as any others on earth, enjoying a stable government, a legal system that is generally just, and a standard of living that is high. Everyday life for most Australians is fundamentally good. How far is it also sacred? Is Australia, a land where 73 percent of people claim to be Christian, in any sense the "south land of the Holy Spirit"?

1. The Dreaming
— and the Nightmare

Until Captain Arthur Phillip led the First Fleet into Sydney harbour in January 1788, the Aborigines had lived on this continent in isolation for more than 40,000 years. The occasional visits of Portuguese, Dutch, Asian and British seafarers in the centuries immediately preceding the British invasion had scarcely touched their way of life. Their complex culture was old long before the pyramids were built in Egypt, or agriculture was pioneered in Anatolia. Theirs was one of the oldest continuous habitations of one people in any place on earth. They lived in a unique and deeply spiritual harmony with their environment, a harmony that grew out of their understanding that the land itself was sacred.

When the First Fleet arrived, estimates suggest that there were probably between 300,000 and 500,000 Aborigines in Australia. Today there are something over 200,000. These figures alone indicate the proportion of the tragedy which European civilization inflicted on a proud and ancient race.

Two hundred years ago, the Aborigines were nomadic hunters and gatherers who lived well most of the time. Their care of their hunting grounds and of their game, and their seasonal patterns of migration, ensured sufficient food despite the harsh and capricious nature of the Australian climate. They exercised a gentle mastery over an environment that white people would find alien and bewildering. They understood it intimately, knowing where to find food and water in places which seemed to be barren. Early white settlers and explorers died of thirst or starvation in places where Aborigines lived in relative prosperity. But their stone-age weaponry would offer them no protection against the nation which ruled half the world.

Central to Aboriginal life was the Dreaming. It was the reality from which all life was derived, not merely an event in the distant past. Time was circular, not linear, as each generation relived the Dreaming activities. Both ritual and daily life were integral to this present reality. For Aborigines there was no division between the sacred and the secular. The sacredness was embodied in the land itself, and particularly in sacred sites and objects — hills, trees, caves, rocks. Each separate group had its own special sacred sites, sacred totems, songs and ceremonies. The stories of the ancestral spirit beings were passed on from one generation to another in the songs, and through a vast oral tradition. The stories had an immediate, practical application as

At many Aboriginal sacred sites, paintings tell the story of events in the "Dreaming" (Coo-ee Picture Library).

well. For they provided rules and warnings for society, and carried information about the environment and its care. Theirs was a highly complex and all-embracing spirituality. Under its gentle care, Australia was truly a land of the Spirit.

The first white observers saw none of this. Seeing no forms of worship that fitted their expectations, they assumed there were none. But in fact traditional Aboriginal culture had a rich variety of religious manifestations. Everyone was involved in some way in the rituals, though some were restricted to men only, or to women only, or to the older members of the group. There was, however, no priestly caste, which obviously confused Christians used to hierarchy. Nor did the blinkered observers realize that religious knowledge was the most valuable possession of all in this culture which set little store by material goods.

The white settlers were further confused by the rich diversity between groups. For at the time of white settlement, Aboriginal society was divided into many different tribal groupings, speaking more than 300 different languages and many more dialects.

Nor did the newcomers understand the delicate checks and balances which allowed these peoples to co-exist. Inter-tribal relations, though often marked by violence, were based on a well-developed etiquette of courtesy and mutual obligation. Within each grouping, kinship obligations including the sharing of food and possessions had a high priority.

When the First Fleet unloaded its dismal cargo of British convicts in Sydney Cove in 1788, the Aboriginal observers were curious but in many ways apathetic. Their long isolation had left them ignorant of the possibility of invasion. The visitors, carrying with them the assumptions of white, British, Christian supremacy, decided the Aborigines were degraded, shiftless savages totally devoid of culture, religion and morals. So the destruction of 40,000 years of Dreaming within a few brief decades was the tragic outcome of the clash of two vastly different cultures.

For Australia's Aborigines, the Dreaming turned to nightmare in the wake of white settlement. The introduction of exotic diseases such as smallpox, measles and influenza, from which they had no immunity, decimated them. The loss of their traditional hunting grounds caused widespread hunger. The white settlers, if they cared at all for the native population, simply assumed that in such a vast country, the Aborigines would be able to move on to other areas to hunt and gather. They had no understanding of the complex territorial divisions which controlled tribal movements. The displaced Aborigines were thus faced with either starvation or tribal warfare.

Worse, Aboriginal women were forcibly abducted, molested and raped. Many suffered horribly. The retaliation of their men folk was interpreted as criminal violence, and heavily punished. The spread of venereal disease affected vast numbers of the Aboriginal population. At the frontiers of white settlement as it moved inexorably across the continent, the level of bloodshed was almost certainly higher than the (white) records show. The cumulative effects on traditional Aboriginal society were traumatic. A culture which had survived all manner of natural and climatic disasters over thousands of years was rapidly undermined. Most surviving Aborigines had no alternative but to work for their new white masters, often under brutal and degrading conditions. Their "payment" — white flour, sugar, tea, alcohol and tobacco — destroyed what physical health they had left. So catastrophic were the cumulative effects of white invasion that many colonists assumed that Aborigines were a dying race, doomed to rapid extinction. For many years, this seemed indeed to be their fate. Only in recent decades has the decline been reversed, and Aboriginal numbers are now on the increase.

With a few honourable exceptions, the leaders of the Christian churches in the Australian colonies failed to champion the cause of the victimized Aboriginal people. Only rarely did Christians speak out publicly in their defence. Too often, they colluded with the notion that Britain was destined to rule this new land. The destruction of the Aboriginal way of life, even of the race itself, was seen as the inevitable consequence of that destiny. Indeed, some saw it as praiseworthy, believing that the "heathen" ways of the defiant black people were to be eradicated at all costs. Understandably, Judeo-Christian morality was offended by practices such as polygamy and infanticide in some areas. They failed to understand the survival realities that made the latter a necessary evil, or to recognize the profound spiritual reality which supported this ancient, if alien, culture.

Even missionaries who had the best interests of the Aborigines at heart nevertheless assumed that the gospel and European civilization were inseparable. The converted Aborigine was expected to abandon all vestiges of traditional life. It must be said, however, in defence of many hard-working Christian missionaries, that they often stood between Aborigines and the murderous intents of unscrupulous white settlers. Without them, in many parts of Australia, Aborigines and their culture may well have been totally eradicated as they were in the island state of Tasmania by the mid-1840s. Many in Australia's Christian denominations today are concerned to redress the failures of the past.

Tragic as this story is, it is one that few white Australians have known anything about until recent years. Black people figured as little more than part of the picturesque backdrop to the triumphs of British settlement in school history books. Aborigines and their extraordinary cultural achievements were of minimal interest to white Australia.

Convicts and soldiers

If the coming of white settlement was a nightmare for Aborigines, it was hardly less so for the first generation of

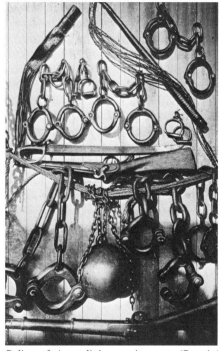

Relics of Australia's convict past (Beattie/ Coo-ee Picture Library).

British colonists in Australia. The First Fleet carried 548 male convicts and 188 female convicts into Sydney harbour, together with a complement of marines to guard them. They had sailed for 252 days across 15,000 miles of ocean, often confined in the ships' fetid holds. The convicts ranged in age from a nine-year-old chimney sweep to an eighty-two-year-old woman; their offences from petty theft to forgery and highway robbery. They were banished into exile on the other side of the world for seven years, or fourteen years, or even for life. They were the first of the 160,000 convicts who would be sent to the Australian colonies before transportation ended in 1868.

For most of this century, Australian historians have been engaged in a lively debate about Australia's convict pioneers. Were they mainly political prisoners like the Tolpuddle Martyrs, transported in 1834 for trade union activities? Were they merely destitute innocents, transported for the theft of a loaf of bread or a handkerchief? Or were they in fact hardened, professional criminals given to debauchery and wickedness of all kinds? Were they unemployed illiterates, or skilled tradespeople? The answer is probably that all these categories were included in their ranks over the eight decades of transportation, in different proportions at different times.

The debate itself has been an important indicator of the formation of Australia's national identity. Until early this century, an eerie silence surrounded the convict beginnings. Most Australians, many of them at that stage descendants of convicts, wanted to forget the past. Convict ancestry was vehemently denied, and for good reasons. Many positions, particularly in the public service, were closed to both ex-convicts and their sons. Politically and personally, colonists strove to camouflage the past by adopting a conventional respectability.

Exiled from home and family perhaps forever, the first convict arrivals and their guards found their new land anything but a compensation. Everything about it was alien, from the stone-age Aboriginal people to the inverted seasons, from the weird birds and animals to the scrubby eucalyptus trees which never lost their leaves. This was truly the known world turned upside down. Though fascinating to the few early visitors with scientific curiosity, it was merely dismal and uninviting to its first reluctant white inhabitants.

And it yielded little response to their attempts at cultivation. In a country where the Aboriginal inhabitants were well fed, the colonists lived on the verge of starvation for five years. During the first two years, their very survival was at stake as the imported crops failed, the stores ran perilously low, and no supply ships rounded the Heads of Sydney harbour. More fleets of convicts, many of them seriously ill from the effects of the arduous voyage and the cruelty of the sadistic commercial contractors who controlled these subsequent journeys, were dumped in Sydney as the colony struggled desperately to feed itself. By the year 1800, only twenty free settlers had come to the new land.

Little wonder few free people were attracted. This continent was settled by the British first and foremost as a jail. Life was harsh, and meant to be so, if transportation was to be a deterrent to criminals back home. In the isolation of Australia, or New South Wales as it was then called, convicts did not have to be locked up. They were not regularly in irons or flogged in Sydney town or its satellite settlements. But the inverted antipodean world far from civilization inevitably bred an inversion of the moral and social values which, at least theoretically, prevailed at home.

Rum, usually of a cheap and fiery kind, governed the early colony. Most people drank to drown their misery. The universal alcoholism led to more misery, from drunken brawls and petty crime to the brutalization of the women. The women's position was extremely difficult. Of the 160,000 convicts transported to Australia, only 25,000 were women, a grave imbalance which could not fail to imprint a profound gender distortion on the new nation's formative years. Consequently few of the convict women had any choice but to become the mistresses or de facto wives of officers, soldiers or other convicts. When the convict ships docked, the women's favours were distributed to the eager sex-starved colonists in what was little more than a degrading shipboard slave market. Soon many of them were enslaved, too, to rum. So the early stereotype of convict women as nothing but degraded whores was engraved on the colony's psyche. It would prove a persistent stereotype, one that would ensure that Australian women were treated at worst harshly, at best dismissively, by generations of Australian men.

Their sentence done, most convicts stayed on in the colony, making new and generally respectable lives for themselves and their families. Only a few went on to amass substantial fortunes themselves. But the children and grandchildren of the convicts became the backbone of a nation. Statistics show that these first-generation Australians were a law-abiding, hard-working people, with a ready love for the native land their parents had found so bewildering and unattractive. The supposed inherited stain of criminality was transparently absent, as the new generation took advantage of the opportunities the new land offered.

The end of the "system", and its legacy

With the growing number of emancipists (freed convicts) and their free-born children, came a growing rate of voluntary emigration to the colony. The combination of free, or almost free, land and free labour meant that those who could stay sober could make a very comfortable living. Increasingly, emigration became an attractive proposition to resourceful Britons frustrated by the limited possibilities available to them at home. The days of the jail were numbered even before British reformers began agitating for an end to the transportation system and all its evils in the 1830s. They were joined in their efforts by the colonists themselves, eager to rid their new home of its criminal reputation. By 1840, transportation to New South Wales had ceased, though it was to continue in Van Diemen's Land (Tasmania) and the infant colony of Western Australia until 1853 and 1868 respectively.

But the "system", as it was called, left its mark, a mark that is still part of Australia's national psyche. The convict founders of white Australia did not bequeath a legacy of criminal predisposition, of rebelliousness, or of moral degradation to the new nation, as early moralists once feared. Australians are as law-abiding, as obedient to authority, and as morally upright as their British cousins. In fact, the sustained effort to overcome a dubious ancestry has probably ensured a commitment to a social, political and moral code of conformity that is out of step with the free and easy life-style of the warm, wide land.

But the convict inheritance is there, nonetheless. It lies beneath the "fair go" philosophy that fiercely resents personal injustices and the denial of reasonable treatment to individuals. It undergirds the deep-seated suspicion of authority figures, be they police or politicians, that marks Australian public life. It can be found in the classlessness that differentiates Australian society from its British parent. The convict transports included all kinds and conditions of men and women, from clergymen, lawyers, architects and gentry to illiterate unemployed labourers, all thrown together. They were powerful equalizers! More importantly, however, the convict origins of the colony meant that few members of the English upper classes were attracted to Australia in its formative years. The harmless, cheeky insubordination that marked much convict conversation and repartee has carried through into modern times in the strand of "larrikinism" that is a unique feature of many levels of Australian life, from everyday humour to religious art ("larrikinism" in this context means a mischievous, generally good-humoured disdain for conventional forms). Many believe that the much-vaunted Australian male code of friendship known as "mateship", which expects a man to stand by his special friend or "mate" through thick and thin, may have originated in convict life. Many male convicts could only have survived the hardships of transportation through this form of mutual help.

It has left less attractive legacies as well. The "stain" of the brutal early years reappears in the dismissive treatment of women as little more than sex objects by many Australian men. This remains, in many respects, a "man's country", a powerfully patriarchal society where women's status is generally lower than in comparable Western countries. The persistent racism that undergirds the attitudes of many Anglo-Celtic Australians can in part be traced back to the convict disdain for the Aborigines, as terrorized convicts in turn terrorized a group of people even more helpless than themselves. In a society where there were relatively few women, particularly on isolated properties or in the penal outstations like Norfolk Island, homosexual practices also flourished in the early years. In many cases, they were part of the convicts' internal system of peer intimidation and control. These practices were so feared and loathed that they may well be one of the sources of the strong homophobia that is still evident in Australia.

The creation of a secular society

The stridency of its harsh penal days still survives under the surface of the great cosmopolitan city that Sydney has become. Bold, brash and hedonistic, its particular psyche is that of a dominant, masculine culture. It differs markedly from gentler, more refined Melbourne, a city founded entirely by free settlers and emancipists. The major Christian churches are an interesting reflection of these differences. In Sydney, they tend to be more conservative than their counterparts in Melbourne. Where Melbourne churches are most often liberal, progressive and ecumenically minded, Sydney's are not always so. The churches' tendency to be puritanical in Sydney may well be a historical reaction to the hedonism that has always flourished around them.

These hallmarks of the Sydney churches reveal most clearly the great divorce between institutionalized religion and Australian life generally. Australia's culture is publicly secular; spirituality is a private matter.

White Australia was not founded by the equivalent of the American Pilgrim Fathers. The new land was not a refuge for a dispossessed and persecuted Christian minority, except in isolated instances. The early Lutheran settlers in South Australia, for instance, were in flight from religious persecution. Rather, modern Australia began as a jail designed to punish, rather than reform, its hapless inmates. In this context, it would have been surprising if the representatives of religion had been given any other role than that of providing moral support for the policing role. And that is exactly what happened.

After representations by prominent Evangelicals, and principally the reformer William Wilberforce, the Rev. Richard Johnson, an Evangelical Anglican clergyman, was appointed chaplain to the new gaol and sailed with the First Fleet. The role of chaplain to Sydney Cove was the toughest job in the Church of England. Johnson was a recent graduate, a man in his early thirties with only limited pastoral experience. He would not be a free agent, answerable only to God and the bishop, as his formal letter of appointment made it clear that he was to obey the orders of the governor of the colony and of any other superior officers, "according to the rules and discipline of war". He was, therefore, firmly part of the "system", and all that that implied, from the very beginning.

Once appointed, Mr Johnson would have sailed virtually empty-handed if it had not been for the Society for the Propagation of the Gospel. This body provided him with a substantial collection of printed materials, ranging from 100 Bibles and Books of Common Prayer (the Anglican standard of worship) to a variety of high-minded tracts. We can only wonder how popular the 100 copies of "Exhortations to Chastity" were in the rum-soaked depravity of early Sydney!

On Australian soil, Mr Johnson found little support for the promotion of religion. No doubt preoccupied with the immense problems of just keeping the infant colony from starvation, its leaders were not much concerned about church buildings. Governor Phillip's orders had included the enforcement of "a due observance of religion", with the provision of whatever was necessary for the celebration of public worship. But a church building was well down on the list of priorities, so worship had to be held in the open air for the first five years of the colony.

That might on occasion have been a pleasant experience, but Sydney's climate is variable, and subject to a high rainfall. In summer, the worshippers baked in the relentless sun; in winter they could be drenched to the skin. Little wonder that few of the colonists — convicts or military — attended. Finally, in 1793, Mr Johnson built a simple house of worship at his own expense, only to see it burnt to the ground by an arsonist in 1798. The firing of Australia's first church was the direct result of government orders for better church attendance and "a more sober and orderly manner of spending the Sabbath Day". No single incident in Australia's white past reflects so dramatically the fierce resistance to enforced public religious observance in this society. A replacement building was a long time in coming.

Among Mr Johnson's duties were those of civil magistrate. In this way, he and his immediate successors found themselves caught up directly in the process of law and order. Clergymen in England regularly undertook the role of magistrate, but in a prison society, under military rule, this position inevitably led to the Christian church being regarded as just another arm of the dreaded "system". The humane ruling that convicts assigned to private settlers could only be flogged by order of a magistrate, meant that clergy became directly involved in the physical punishment of the convicts to whom they were supposed to be ministering.

The "flogging parson"

The most famous — or infamous — example of the clergyman magistrate was the Rev. Samuel Marsden, known to history as the "flogging parson". Marsden, the stocky son of a Yorkshire butcher, was another Evangelical Anglican protegee of Wilberforce. Newly ordained, he was appointed assistant chaplain to the colony of New South Wales in 1793. From the beginning, this keen, energetic Evangelical was frustrated by the total indifference of his new flock. He preached not just to deaf ears but to largely absent ears. He would undertake a number of highly successful missionary journeys to New Zealand to compensate for the stony indifference he found in his new land. Evidently he was a man better suited to being a missionary than a convict chaplain, for his memory is held in high respect on the other side of the Tasman. But in New South Wales, as magistrate, Marsden became tragically involved in the two feeble uprisings of Irish convicts. The Irish, many of them sentenced to transportation for their part in rebellions against English rule in Ireland, formed a large proportion of the convict numbers in early New South Wales. They were, from the beginning, treated especially harshly, feared as they were not only for their propensity to insurrection but also for their fierce adherence to the Roman Catholic faith. In this ecumenical age, it is easy to forget the deep antipathy that loyal Britishers, until very recently, felt towards Catholicism, the legacy of the bitterness of the sixteenth-century Protestant Reformation in Britain.

Marsden's bigotry was, unfortunately, typical of his generation. To him the Irish were a "savage race... destitute of every Principle of Religion & Morality". They were treacherous criminals of the worst kind. So when rumours of uprising came to him in 1800, Marsden and other magistrates did not hesitate to sentence the suspects to severe floggings. In particular, he ordered what amounted to savage torture by the flogging of one suspect, in the vain hope of extracting information from him. Even in brutalized New South Wales, the parson's behaviour then and on subsequent similar occasions was regarded by some as scandalous.

Nor did Marsden have any sympathy with the Irish plea for Catholic worship. An offer by two Catholic priests to join the First Fleet and minister to its Catholic convicts had been rejected, and requests over the years that convict-priests be permitted to celebrate the mass were similarly refused by the colonial authorities. Finally, in 1803, Father James Dixon, a convict, was permitted to celebrate both the mass and a marriage in Sydney. He was then permitted to say mass each Sunday. Marsden was disgusted, and was firmly convinced that this misguided leniency was the direct cause of an ill-fated Irish rebellion in 1804. Allowing the Irish convicts to come together for mass gave agitators a golden opportunity to plot rebellion, he claimed. Far better, he argued, for all Catholic worship to be denied, and the Irish forced to attend Protestant services. He hoped in this way that Catholicism would soon die out in the colony. He got his way for a short while, as no further public Catholic worship was allowed in New South Wales after the uprising until 1820. In that year, in advance of Catholic emancipation in Britain, two Catholic chaplains took up their official appointment to the colony, paid for by the British government. Soon after, work commenced on the first Roman Catholic church in Sydney.

Marsden, harsh and uncompromising in his religious views, was a controversial character. And yet he is remembered across the Tasman as an outstanding missionary, he had a high reputation in early Sydney as a farmer, and was a founder of the Australian wool industry. Unlike most of the early colonists, he quickly came to love his adopted land, declaring it to be one of the finest countries in the known world. He was a man of contradictions, and so demonstrates on an exaggerated scale the white response to this land of contradictions.

His legacy to the future Australian church can only be described as tragic, for the legend of the "flogging parson" ensured a lasting bitterness towards institutionalized religion. His behaviour compromised the church for decades, and cemented the ancient hatred between the English and Irish, between Protestant and Catholic, on the other side of the world. He is symbolic of the attitudes and mistakes on the part of the Christian churches which helped in the creation of secular Australia.

It was not merely their experiences of transportation that hardened the convicts against religious teaching. Secular Australia may have been brought to birth under southern skies, but it was conceived in England. In the late eighteenth century, the Church of England had completely failed to reach the urban masses — the poor, ordinary men and women of the crowded cities. Long before they set sail for Botany Bay, the convicts were known to be an irreligious lot, some felt even an irredeemable lot. They were impervious to religious teaching, or to encouragement to prayer or worship. Thus they — and to a certain extent the soldiers and free settlers who came largely from the same class — brought with them to Australia the godlessness of the hidden side of English life. Transportation, and the church's collusion in it, simply magnified and entrenched this indifference.

The faith of the Irish

Ironically, in contrast to the godlessness of the English, Irish convicts longed for the comfort of their faith. While Johnson and Marsden bewailed their tiny congregations, the Irish begged for the mass. Without priests, some of them maintained faithful, private religious devotion. So while the Church of England transplanted a formal Protestant ascendancy in Australia, it was Irish men and women who sought the comfort of the Holy Spirit under the Southern Cross.

Australia's first two official Roman Catholic priests, Philip Conolly and John Joseph Therry, arrived to find a well-organized Catholic community, solidly refusing to yield to the Anglican establishment. Many of Sydney's first Catholics would not marry or have their children baptized according to Anglican rites, thus no doubt fuelling the claims of Marsden and his friends that the Irish were an immoral lot! Conolly moved on to Hobart, where in fact there were few Catholics, and his ministry was not a success story. Therry, on the other hand, found himself with a potential congregation of many thousands, as Catholics were by then almost a quarter of Sydney's population. Irish convicts were always transported direct to Sydney, thereby establishing from the beginning a strong Irish element in Sydney's racial mix. Until very recently, the Australian Catholic church was markedly Irish in its character. Therry, though a controversial character who disputed readily with the authorities and with numbers of his own flock, and who, like Marsden, built himself a substantial empire of land holdings, nevertheless left a good reputation behind him. His pastoral care for his people was long remembered.

The very early period left an indelible mark on Australian Catholicism. The refusal to allow regular Catholic worship for the first thirty-two years was deeply resented. The growing number of Catholic colonists felt discriminated against, even persecuted. Without doubt, this experience helped build up a consolidated Catholic defensiveness against what they saw as a hostile Protestant society. It became part of the folk-memory of a significant minority group.

Their defensiveness was justified, for anti-papal feeling ran strongly in the colony. Marsden was certainly not alone in his opinions. Governor Darling's attempt to establish an interdenominational school system foundered when Anglicans joined other Protestants in condemning the proposal. The notion that Catholics should have a part in the colony's education programme horrified them. That defeat, too, was prophetic. Sectarian differences bedevilled every attempt to create a comprehensive educational system for the rest of the nineteenth century. Governments were ultimately forced into providing totally secular education as a result.

The Irish Catholics were not the only religious minority in early New South Wales. The first Nonconformists came by accident. Missionaries with the London Missionary Society, they fled to Sydney from danger in Tahiti in 1798. Marsden, with his Evangelical Anglican background, welcomed them and soon had them at work, teaching and preaching in the colony. Likewise, he was very supportive, at least at first, of Samuel Leigh, the first Methodist preacher sent to the colony in 1815. However, not all the Methodists liked the Sydney Anglican clergy, finding their commitment to Calvinism rather disturbing.

The first Presbyterian minister was the Rev. Dr John Dunmore Lang, a man of steel who never flinched from controversy and dissension. He became embroiled in controversy as soon as he arrived in Sydney in 1823. He was furious that the then governor, Thomas Brisbane, wanted to treat Presbyterians patronisingly as dissenters. He forcefully reminded Brisbane that most Presbyterians were from the Church of Scotland, itself an established church in the British Isles. He won, and gained both a government stipend for himself and funding for the building of a church. Significantly, he also gained the right to perform marriages, thus ending the monopoly of the Anglican church. It was only in 1855 that clergy of all denominations were allowed to celebrate marriages.

There was also, from the beginning, a small Jewish community. At least four Jews were among the First Fleet convicts. Their numbers had increased sufficiently by the 1840s for their leaders to agitate for government financial assistance with the cost of their Sydney synagogue, and the stipend for their rabbi. But Jews were even farther from the standards of the Church of England than Catholics, and they received a generally unsympathetic hearing. The Jewish community in Australia has remained relatively small, accounting for only about half of one percent of the population. Though Australia has known periods of appalling racism, Jews have not suffered from a high level of specific discrimination in this country. Rather, Aborigines and Asians have been the traditional targets of racist propaganda.

Church and state

Despite the existence of a large degree of religious diversity in the colony, the Church of England assumed that its place in the life of the settlement was to be the same as it was in England — the "established", or state, church. For the first few decades, that was indeed its de facto position, with its chaplains appointed as officers of the crown. But the colony quickly outgrew its prison beginnings. How were future clergy to be appointed and paid in the new, free settlements? For a brief time, it looked as if the Anglicans would be given substantial financial priority, with the provision of large tracts of lands through a church and schools corporation. But this anachronistic move was short-lived, as the other Protestants, the Roman Catholics and the colony's landed "gentry" combined to oppose this special privilege. It was soon abandoned, and by the time the first Anglican bishop of Australia, William Grant Broughton, was appointed in 1836, "establishment" for the Church of England was a dead letter.

In the same year, a "church act" gave the main denominations equality before the law, salaries for their clergy, and subsidies for their church buildings. Because of the conditions of the funding, the Church of England maintained its earlier advantages. And it would continue to maintain, too, a symbolic priority. To this day, it commands an influence in the community that is disproportionate to its worshipping numbers. The 1836 act also maintained the link between church and state, effectively "establishing" all the main denominations. Such a high level of support for institutional religion was not popular with many in the colonies, where strong anti-clerical feeling flourished among some intellectuals as well as the working classes.

Nor did the financial assistance actually do much good for the churches. The government handouts effectively gave great power to denominational leaders. The bishops of the Anglican and Roman Catholic churches especially were seen to have great patronage at their disposal. They could, and sometimes did, behave autocratically with the power of the purse strings so solidly in their hands. Inevitably, the colonial government found itself being drawn into disputes over the right use of the money it distributed. And the churches themselves, where once there had been a fair degree of ecumenical co-operation, were soon involved in unseemly squabbles and outright competition. So there was relief all round when the various colonial legislatures, in the second half of the nineteenth century, abolished this divisive form of state aid. The churches were then free to restore their earlier partnership, at least among the Protestants. Roman Catholics remained well beyond the pale for most!

Bound for South Australia

South Australia, on the other hand, was an Australian colony deliberately founded to avoid the strong influence of the Anglican hierarchy, established or not. This colony was neither a

From the start a colony for free settlers, South Australia offered religious equality to "dissenters" still disadvantaged under English law. This drawing of Adelaide's first Congregational Church is dated 1837 (Coo-ee Picture Library).

convict prison nor an offshoot of one. It was originally promoted by a company, the South Australian Land Company, set up by a coalition of interested individuals and parties in England in 1832. They wanted to establish a colony in this promising but so far unsettled part of the continent where free men and women could live and work and prosper in virtuous harmony. They would be protected from the sin and depravity of convicts and others of bad character. And most importantly, here there would be no state church. Those "dissenters" (Methodists, Congregationalists, Baptists and the like) who were still disadvantaged under English law, would find religious equality and freedom. There would be a complete separation of church and state. With the official approval of the British colonial office, the first settlers arrived in South Australia in 1836.

The high ideals of the first South Australians did not survive long in the reality of the hardships of the colony's first years. The settlement was torn by division and argument. By 1846, the ideals had so far disappeared that the major church bodies asked for — and received — state aid for religion, much to the dismay of others. Inevitably, it just caused further problems, as it had in the other colonies. And despite its dissenting origins, South Australia soon had a majority of Anglicans. It had only a mere handful of Roman Catholics, however, so Protestantism was in the ascendancy.

Among the Protestants were a group of pious Lutherans from Prussia, attracted by the prospect of religious freedom. They, and other German settlers who followed them, added a new dimension to the overwhelmingly Anglo-Celtic Australian colonies. Their influence continues, visible in the pretty German townships which still dot the Adelaide Hills. They brought to the southern continent not only a European style of Protestantism, but also the German art of grape-growing and wine-making, for which this part of South Australia is renowned.

The die is cast

So by the middle of the nineteenth century, the major religious traditions of the British Isles were firmly transplanted in the great south land of the Holy Spirit. The Church of England, stripped of special status on the other side of the world, nevertheless retained an ascendancy of influence. Generally,

Anglicans and other British Protestants shared a good working relationship, though they too often succumbed to the temptation to unite in opposition to the Roman Catholic Church. A substantial, Irish-dominated church, it would carry for many generations the bitter memory of its earlier discrimination, and feed on the far more bitter memories of the long English occupation of Ireland. In turn, the Protestants perpetuated under southern skies their long folk-memory of anti-Roman fear and prejudice.

Alongside the degrading interdenominational squabbles, most Australians continued on the path of secularism and anti-clericalism. Formal religion remained at best something quite peripheral. And the Aborigines, as they suffered the destruction not only of their culture but of their very lives, received little from the influence of Christianity. The British churches were not interested in specific missionary endeavours among the continent's Aboriginal people, and the local clergy were fully occupied trying to minister to their godless white flock. They generally showed little concern for the disintegrating black society on the edges of their own world. The few missions that were attempted in the early period failed dismally, not least because they readily assumed that the Christian gospel was synonymous with English civilization and the Protestant work ethic. In their ignorance, they tried to convert to their European version of the Holy Spirit, a people who had held in sacred trust the land of the Holy Spirit for 40,000 years.

2. Building a Nation

In a remarkably short period of time, the brutal penal colony on the edge of starvation was transformed into a land of hope and opportunity. But that came about largely because of an upsurge in free settlement.

The same hardships and community dislocation in Britain that had thrown up generations of convicts also produced vast numbers of poverty-stricken but honest men and women chafing at the narrow horizons of their future. Many English people lived in squalor, and went to bed hungry every night of their lives. To provide even a bare subsistence, children as young as eight years old worked long and dangerous hours in mines and factories. Far more destitute were the Scottish and Irish rural families driven from their lands and livelihoods by rapacious landlords or years of famine. The one hope for a reasonable life lay in emigration.

The British government saw emigration as an answer to its population explosion, while in Sydney itself a growing number of men and women believed that assisting free settlers to emigrate was the only means of overcoming the convict stain. Some of them, people of means, had themselves emigrated earlier, in the hope of making an even larger fortune in the new world. Besides, the supply of convict labour was, by the 1830s, no longer adequate; a larger labour force was essential if the country's agricultural industries were to develop.

So it was that the British government began a scheme of assisted emigration to New South Wales and Tasmania in 1831. The aim was to increase the labour force in the colonies without increasing the already serious imbalance between the sexes. So single women and families were particularly encouraged to try their luck in the new world. Those who took up the opportunity of self-betterment in this way were the more ambitious and resourceful of the rural and urban working classes; records show that almost half the adult emigrants of this time could read, and that a large proportion of them could write as well, a significantly high proportion of literacy for this group in society.

Conditions aboard the emigrant ships bound for Australia were harsh and uncomfortable. But at least the long, tedious voyage was not as dangerous as the much shorter trip to North America, thanks to the high level of government involvement in the Australian emigration system. Government interest ensured not only that shipping safety was of a far higher standard than on the unregulated Atlantic crossing, but also that there were far fewer opportunities for rogues to rob gullible passengers of their precious savings. Nevertheless, some 2500 hopeful Britishers drowned at sea on their way to the new south land, their great adventure ended in shipwreck.

Life in Australia was not immediately rewarding for the "new chums". Single women and families were not in great demand on the distant rural farm holdings. Property owners did not want to house and keep whole families; what they wanted was single men. So many of the new arrivals found themselves living under tents in Sydney's open spaces, their precious savings disappearing as they waited for employment. The single girls were the most disadvantaged. Without protectors, destitute young women were too often lured into prostitution for their very survival.

The "emigrants' friend"

Neither the government nor the churches endeavoured to correct this chaotic situation. Instead, it was a devout, determined woman who, virtually unaided, changed the face of Australian emigration. Caroline Chisholm, born in 1808 into an Evangelical Anglican family who farmed near Northampton, England, became a Roman Catholic on her marriage to an officer of the East India Company. On leave from India, the Chisholms came to Sydney in 1838. Horrified by the plight of the immigrants, particularly of the single women, Caroline set about changing the situation. She met every immigrant ship, becoming a familiar figure on the wharves of Sydney town. She took some girls into her own home, and found work for others. After much persuasion and despite anti-Catholic feeling directed against her plans, she finally convinced the governor and his wife of the need for a female immigrant shelter.

Next she helped move the immigrants into jobs in the country. She herself often travelled into the bush with the nervous newcomers. Later, she returned to Britain to tackle reform of the whole emigration system. When her attempts to enlist government support failed, she set up her own emigration society in 1849. She agitated for many other reforms, including the ready availability of good land for small, independent farmers in Australia. She is remembered as the "emigrant's friend", the title engraved on her gravestone in her native Northampton.

Attractive, personable, a devoted wife and mother and a devout Christian, this fearless radical is the great heroine of nineteenth-century Australia. She is the only woman — apart from the British sovereign — to have been featured on Australian currency. Her portrait is on the $5 note. Her contribution to Australian life and welfare is scarcely typical, but it is symbolic of the nature of some of the most effective Christian influence in this country. Devout, determined people such as Caroline have sometimes been greater witnesses to the faith than the churches to which they owed their allegiance. The Christian story in Australia is, in many respects, the story of remarkable individuals who often achieved results despite the churches. In Caroline's case, she did not at first receive wholehearted support from her own church, and yet her identification with Catholicism provided a ready excuse for some Protestants to oppose her.

Sydney's controversial first Presbyterian minister, John Dunmore Lang, was another strong supporter of emigration to Australia. Unlike Mrs Chisholm, however, emigration for him was a means of curbing what he saw as the disturbing growth of Roman Catholicism in the Antipodes. Upright Protestant working men and women would also help remedy the terrible moral depravity of the penal colony, he believed. He recruited numbers of immigrants, many of them Scottish, and undertook extensive lecture tours around the British Isles extolling the virtues of Australian life. He too, like Mrs Chisholm, founded emigration societies which chartered their own ships. But like many of the endeavours of this dynamic but tactless and antagonistic man, his efforts for immigrants were clouded by controversy and misinformation. His memory remains a troubled one for Australian Christians.

Gold!

The biggest boost to Australia's wealth and population came not from earnest hard-working emigrants content to gain a reasonable living in the new world, but from the fortune-seekers who followed the cry, "Gold!" The first gold discovery in Australia was made near Bathurst in western New South Wales

Shearers

No church-bell rings them from the Track.
No pulpit lights their blindness —
'Tis hardship, drought, and homelessness
That teach those Bushmen kindness:
The mateship born, in barren lands,
Of toil and thirst and danger,
The camp-fare for the wanderer set,
The first place to the stranger.

They do the best they can today —
Take no thought of the morrow;
Their way is not the old-world way —
They live to lend and borrow.
When shearing's done and cheques gone wrong,
They call it "time to slither!" —
They saddle up and say "so-long!"
And ride the Lord knows whither.

And though he may be brown or black,
Or wrong man there, or right man,
The mate that's steadfast to his mates
They call that man a "white man!"

Australian Information Service/John McKinnon

They tramp in mateship side by side —
The Protestant and Roman —
They call no biped lord or sir,
And touch their hat to no man!

They carry in their swags, perhaps,
A portrait and a letter —
And, maybe, deep down in their hearts,
The hope of "something better".
Where lonely miles are long to ride,
And long, hot days recurrent,
There's lots of time to think of men
They might have been — but weren't.

They turn their faces to the west
And leave the world behind them
(Their drought-dry graves are seldom set
Where even mates can find them).
They know too little of the world
To rise to wealth or greatness:
But in these lines I gladly pay
My tribute to their straightness.

Henry Lawson, 1867-1922

in 1851. This was soon followed by even more spectacular finds in Victoria, a colony only newly separated from New South Wales. It was Victoria which experienced the most dramatic changes at this time.

Within a decade of the discovery of gold, the population of the colonies had tripled. These new immigrants who flocked to Australia in the hope of making a quick and easy fortune were predominantly young, middle-class, literate and male. They brought with them far more than hope and strong muscles; they brought the many talents and trades that had previously earned them a living in the old world. In the new world, when the lure of gold proved an illusion to many after only a matter of months on the goldfields, they flocked into Australia's cities. There they established a variety of factories, workshops and other entrepreneurial activities which quickly broadened the base of the country's economy. They became leaders in Australian political and public life in the second half of the nineteenth century.

An enormous quantity of gold was mined in Australia. Millions of pounds' worth was exported in the boom years, vastly increasing the wealth of the colonies. In the two-year period 1850-52, Victoria's total revenue had increased six-fold. At the peak of the rush, there were 181,000 gold miners in Victoria in 1858. In important ways, the gold rush and its legacy shifted the focus of dynamic growth and development in Australia from Sydney to Melbourne for several decades.

Life on the goldfields was harsh and often primitive. Miners of all classes were soon indistinguishable — unwashed, unshaven, dressed in rough working clothes, as they toiled long hours in all weathers for the elusive metal. Drunkenness, gambling and brawling were common. Once more, this was a man's country. Male mateship was central to survival, let alone success, on the diggings; women were outsiders. Many a wife and family had been left behind to fend for themselves.

Only a very few diggers made fabulous fortunes. The vast majority probably only made reasonable wages; a minority actually left the goldfields poorer than they had arrived. The publicans and store-keepers at the diggings made the most consistent profits. By the late 1850s, many gold-rush immigrants had resumed a more normal life in the cities. The old goldfields, denuded of trees and topsoil, pock-marked by the wholesale, indiscriminate digging, remained an eyesore for generations. They represent some of the worst rape of the land in Australia's sorry history of exploitation of the environment.

Religion had not been totally ignored on the goldfields. Indeed, many observers noted how well the sabbath was respected, so far from anything resembling civilization. Many miners attended services of worship when provided. Coming mostly from the middle classes, they had experienced a greater exposure to Christianity than had most earlier migrants, who had come largely from the poor rural and urban working classes. But the churches, by and large, did not respond quickly to the challenge of gold. By the 1850s they were only just catching up with the earlier waves of immigration. Numbers of church buildings and clergy were only then beginning to be anything like sufficient for the task. And it was a missionary task that faced them. It has been estimated that only one eighth of the Victorian population attended church in the pre-goldrush days.

The Eureka Stockade

The gold rushes, substantially over so far as individual mining was concerned by the 1860s, left a complex legacy for Australia. Such rapid growth and rapid change, combined with an influx of middle class, educated people, could not fail to have a profound impact on colonial society. Though this impact was felt for generations, its most public manifestation was the Eureka Stockade of 1854.

The costs of policing and administering the goldfields in Victoria in the early 1850s were raised by the imposition of prohibitively expensive licence fees on individual diggers. Paid monthly, they were a heavy burden on diggers who were not earning much money from their claims. Naturally, many tried to evade payment, only to be searched out by police, and then fined even more heavily. In 1854, as the goldfields became harder to work and more men fell into debt, the licence system and its often brutal policing became the subject of deep resent-

A scene from the Victorian goldfields, 1852. The "gold rush" accelerated the pace of change in colonial Australia, hastening moves towards ending the convict system, and implementing self-government, democracy and land reform (Coo-ee Picture Library).

ment among diggers. Widespread corruption among goldfields officials further fuelled the diggers' anger.

The situation finally came to a head at Eureka, near Ballarat. Experienced political agitators among the miners had helped the disadvantaged diggers form a reform league, which proposed the abolition of the hated licence system, as well as votes for all adult males and reform of the parliamentary system. But political rights were secondary to the local grievances, which ultimately lit the bonfire. Roused by a confrontation between police and miners over a corrupt murder trial, the miners publicly burnt their licences. With troops fast moving into the area, the miners built a stockade. The 150 or so diggers who finally occupied it had few arms. When the troops suddenly attacked in the middle of the night, they were quickly routed. At least thirty diggers died immediately or from their wounds. The victorious police and soldiers behaved appallingly, shooting and bayonetting the wounded, the prisoners and even some who were innocent bystanders.

It was a tragic, unnecessary episode. The reformed goldfields' administration that was its most positive outcome could have been implemented without bloodshed, if common sense had prevailed among government officials. Instead deliberate provocation ended in the only "revolution" on Australian soil. It was significant that the miners' leader, Peter Lalor, and indeed many of the rebels, were Irish Catholic. A Catholic priest sheltered the wounded Lalor after the debacle. The age-old antipathy between English and Irish, Protestant and Catholic, provided at least some of the context of this revolt against the establishment. The thirteen diggers tried for high treason were all acquitted, and public feeling has always run strongly in favour of the rebels. In a country with few such moments of high drama, Eureka has stood for the triumph of the "little man" against bureaucracy and authority, and a victory for democracy and a "fair go". Undoubtedly, the legend has meant more than the actual event, which some historians have regarded as little more than a farce. The "southern cross" flag the rebel miners devised as a demonstration of their republican sentiments still appears frequently in anti-establishment protests.

The whole gold rush experience, including Eureka, accelerated the pace of change and development in colonial Australia.

It hastened moves towards ending the convict system in eastern Australia, and implementing self-government, democracy and land reform. Ultimately it was the latter which became most important as the disillusioned diggers returned to everyday life after gold had disappointed them.

Racism

The bitterest legacy of the gold rushes was, however, racism. Large numbers of Chinese descended on the goldfields with great rapidity — 18,000 of them within the first eighteen months in Victoria alone. Europeans, particularly Anglo-Celts with virtually no experience of Asia, were suddenly confronted with the alien appearance, culture and customs of the Chinese.

Riot and disorder were the immediate result, as the white miners sought to drive the newcomers away, often violently. The riots led colonial legislatures to pass specific acts restricting Chinese immigration — repealed once the immediate threat was over. As surface gold became rarer, the ability of industrious Chinese to extract a meagre living from reworking old mine sites was resented by less industrious unemployed whites. The Chinese, the white men claimed, were cruel, dishonest, immoral, dirty and treacherous. Convinced of their innate inferiority, the whites nevertheless feared that, because of their sheer numbers and evil cunning, they would soon gain the ascendancy in Australian society. Thus ignorance, panic and naked racism gave birth to the fear of the "yellow peril" that would dominate Australia's relationship with Asia well into the second half of the twentieth century. Its ugliest manifestation was in the last decades of the nineteenth century, long after the gold rushes themselves had ended.

Unlocking the land

From the beginning of white settlement in Australia until the 1820s, the major method of distributing land was by way of free grants. Ignoring the Aborigines, governments assumed they owned the land and could distribute it as they pleased. Emancipated convicts were Australia's first landholders, followed by officers of the New South Wales Corps and free settlers. Many of the smaller settlers, however, sold out to the large landholders, often in the early days for rum.

After 1830, as more free settlers arrived, Australia experienced a great rush to the interior. "Squatters" were settlers who travelled into the untapped interior of the country, and simply "squatted" on land they did not own. They used it principally for grazing, and many of Australia's rich families of the last century owed their wealth to these somewhat irregular beginnings.

With the end of the free grant system in 1831, crown lands were put up for sale. But the price was far too high for people on low wages, so owner-farming remained out of the reach of hopeful immigrants to this land of such vast acres. However, all attempts to make land more accessible failed until the goldrush migration forced government action.

The Eureka Stockade no doubt warned the colonial governments of the dangers of rebellion if some provision was not made for the luckless gold seekers and other immigrants. As each colony now enjoyed full responsible government, the control of crown lands passed to the colonial legislatures. So in the late 1850s and 60s, the cry went up — "unlock the land!" The poor, the landless, the diggers all wanted the opportunity to settle and work small farms of their own. In the egalitarian society of the new world, few wanted to be tenant farmers, let alone farm workers. The great Australian dream of home ownership, a dream which is still the first priority for most families, is an extension of this longing to own one's own patch of land.

There was also a real need to turn more land to agriculture rather than purely pastoral pursuits. Wool might once more be king of the Australian economy, but the expanding population needed to eat. More wheat must be grown, and quickly. So, despite concerted opposition from the squatters and their allies, land acts were passed in Victoria and New South Wales in the 1860s. Many had visions of a strong, independent farming class developing in Australia after all.

But the future was not to be so rosy. "Land sharks" and profiteers of all kinds moved in quickly. Widespread bribery, corruption and criminal practices ensured that few genuine "selectors" gained good land under the terms of the acts. The population of the "bush" did increase, but mostly with a generation of farmers doomed to failure and poverty. Their finances exhausted by the purchase of their small holding, they had no money left to invest in machinery, let alone to cushion them against the vagaries of the harsh Australian climate. There were no drought-resistant strains of wheat available until the 1880s, so many saw their crops perish in the soil in the dry seasons. Even if they enjoyed a bumper harvest, transporting it to the cities was costly. Cheap rail transport did not conquer the Great Dividing Range (the mountains which cut off the narrow coastal strip from the great interior) until much later in the century.

Some settlers managed to succeed despite the great odds against them. Most did not. Few could withstand the recurring Australian extremes of flood, drought and bushfires. Settlers might survive years of drought, only to be ruined by devastating floods, or the terrifying bushfires that sweep across the south-eastern states with unnerving regularity in the dry summer weather. The hardships, isolation and grinding poverty they endured before they finally had no choice but to sell out to the squatters, left a legend of the bush that has become an integral part of Australian folklore. It reinforced the tendency to urbanization, and the fear of the inland that has seen Australians cling so tenaciously to the coastline. The bushrangers who are a part of the Australian bush legend came mostly from the poor settlers. Many began their careers of crime stealing stock from the rich squatters whose prosperity they so much resented. The evocative bush poems and ballads of the late nineteenth century preserve the harsh experiences of rural Australia for all time.

The explorers

These views were reinforced by the efforts of numbers of explorers to chart the vast unknown interior of the continent. Some believed there must be a large inland sea — no doubt ringed by rich, fertile land — at the country's heart. The colony's earliest explorers did open up the valuable lands and rivers of southern Australia. But the later explorers, who ventured into the far interior, were doomed to disappointment. There was no inland sea, only a "dead heart". Some suffered more than disappointment; a number died. The Prussian Ludwig Leichhardt, after a successful trip to the far north, perished in 1848 with all his party on his second attempt to cross the continent from east to west. In 1861, an expedition to the north by Burke and Wills also ended in disaster. Both men died. They, and other more successful explorers, revealed the innate harshness of the Australian continent, and the capriciousness of its climate. They opened up some good land, but also endless drought-stricken plains and deserts.

The churches

The Church of England had already taken steps to deal with the difficulties imposed by its quasi-established position in colonial society before the gold rushes. Most migrants who owed their allegiance to the Church of England did not expect to have to support its work in more than a token way. After all, that was the case in England, where central funds and local endowments paid for the clergy. The church in Australia was also hampered by lack of personnel, as English clergy were less than wiiling to give up their comfortable livings and status at home for the rigours of the bush and the egalitarianism of colonial society. But most serious was the lack of funds.

The first Anglican bishop of Melbourne, Charles Perry, realized that he needed to encourage genuine lay participation and therefore lay responsibility, if the Australian church was to become viable. So he became one of the first to introduce synodical government into the Church of England.

Perry's name is remembered for his remarkable contribution to something akin to democratic government in the Anglican church. It is not, however, revered for ecumenism! Perry, scholarly, resourceful and hard-working, was also a narrow-minded Evangelical. He was forthright in his opinion that Roman Catholics suffered under "a Satanic delusion".

In one of his first actions in the colony after his arrival in 1848, he reversed a pattern of genuine ecumenical sharing between Melbourne's Catholics and Protestants. When the first Catholic chapel was built in the city, Protestants had helped with the fund-raising, and their open-hearted generosity had not been forgotten. The first Roman Catholic priest in the city, Patrick Geoghegan, was a proponent of religious toleration. He was also a courteous man, and so dropped his calling card as a welcome to the newly arrived Bishop Perry. Perry, however, declined to return the call. Writing to Geoghegan, he politely insisted that the theological differences between them would make any social relationship "an occasion of pain rather than pleasure".

Perry's action caused considerable controversy, for Father Geoghegan was well-liked and respected throughout the colony by people of every religious persuasion. He was on friendly terms with the other Protestant clergy. Perry's action and subsequent anti-Roman denunciations imported into Melbourne something of the fierce religious strife in England in the wake of the Catholic emancipation act of 1829 as well as the Anglo-Catholic revival. Anglican-Roman relations in Melbourne did not return to their original goodwill until well into the following century.

The golden age

Overall, the immediate result of the gold rushes in Victoria was a golden age for the churches. Many of the gold-rush migrants had been influenced by Methodism in Britain, particularly in the mining communities of Cornwall and Wales. Methodist lay preachers had also offered an effective church presence on the goldfields. So the gold-towns of Victoria, and coal-mining areas such as Newcastle in New South Wales, became strongholds of "chapel" rather than church. Methodist church buildings dotted the streets of the gold-rush towns.

Three Methodist groups were influential in Australia in the second half of the nineteenth century — the Wesleyans, the Primitive Methodists, and the Bible Christians who were strongest in South Australia. Presbyterianism was also at its height in Victoria in the decades following the gold rushes. It was a rich church, and built many stately church buildings in town and country to prove it! Congregationalism, however, flourished most in New South Wales and South Australia.

In Victoria in particular, all the churches enjoyed good attendance figures in this period. Two-thirds of the adult population went to church regularly, and Sunday school figures were at an all-time high. It must be remembered that this was the era of the family and of the growth of the rural population. After so many decades of male-female imbalance, the numbers of the sexes were now more equal, and Australian society at last was looking less like a male frontier under the impact of domesticity. The land acts had populated the bush, and so built up the country towns, particularly in Victoria. Rural families are more likely to be churchgoers than single city-dwellers.

Historians have also pointed out the importance of religion for this large migrant population. The Presbyterian Church functioned very much as a Scottish community, the Roman Catholic Church as an Irish friendly society. English migrants tended to find like-minded people in the Anglican and Methodist churches. Most migrants remained true to their home churches, but some Nonconformists changed their allegiance to the Church of England as they became wealthy and made their way up the social ladder. The Church of England was still regarded as the Establishment at prayer.

But Christianity in Australia was largely planted by homesick people. Their religious practices remained fiercely conservative despite the democratic egalitarianism of wider Australian life. Visitors to Australia commented frequently on this conservatism, and in particular on the extreme Englishness of Methodist and Anglican worship. Any who looked for a genuine Australian religiosity were doomed to disappointment. It seemed almost as if the overwhelming experiences of life in the wide brown land left religion untouched; indeed, as if religion itself remained strangely aloof from its influence. So Australia developed no home-grown varieties of Christianity as happened so readily in the United States. It would find a place for a few American denominations and sects — the Churches of Christ and the Mormons are good examples — but on the whole, Christianity in Australia to this day is concentrated largely in the major churches. Only in recent years has the growing popularity of Pentecostal churches begun to challenge that situation.

Wherever a small country township sprang up in the years of expansion in the second half of last century, churches were built. Sometimes, given the distances involved and the lack of capital, Protestants of varying traditions would combine to build one church and employ one clergyman. Most bush people were happy to receive religious rites at the hands of clergy of any denomination. But the union churches were the remarkable exceptions to the general rule. Mostly, churches of each of the major denominations sprang up along the town's main street. Lay people, usually the women, struggled to raise the necessary funds to keep "their" church afloat. For many living in outlying districts, or in the far outback, churchgoing was a rare event. But in many a bush home, a family Bible was a treasured possession, and many an overworked mother took time to ensure that her growing family knew at least the basic Christian story.

Across country towns and in the cities, as European civilization was built out of nothing, much that would make Australian life gentler and kinder was pioneered by devout Christian individuals. Behind the hospitals and benevolent societies, the orphanages and charities were selfless hardworking lay people who were inspired as much by their faith as by their sense of duty. But often as not, their faith remained a private matter, something rarely recorded in the history books.

Religious orders

More public and obvious was the contribution of the Roman Catholic religious orders. The first, five Irish Sisters of Charity, arrived in Sydney in 1838 to begin a pastoral ministry among convicts, the sick, and orphans. They also undertook teaching activities. They went on to found Australia's first major hospital, St Vincent's.

Teaching orders of nuns followed. Often they had to raise all their own funds and battle intrusive, autocratic bishops as well. Mother Vincent Whitty, superior of a convent of Sisters of Mercy in Brisbane, was a dynamic activist who built many schools in Queensland. But the domineering Bishop James Quinn, who insisted on complete authority over every aspect of the sisters' lives and work, actually dismissed her from office in 1865, and deprived her of the right to speak in chapter meetings.

Increasingly, religious orders were needed to take over the rapidly-growing Catholic parish school system. So between 1880 and 1910, the number of teaching sisters throughout Australia multiplied more than five times, increasing from 815 to more than 5,000. They included the local order, the Sisters of St Joseph of the Sacred Heart, which had been founded in Adelaide in 1867. It became the largest religious congregation in Australia. Today, there are more than 13,000 women and men in Australia's Roman Catholic religious orders and congregations, facing the same challenges in the post-Vatican II era as their counterparts in other countries.

The Sisters of St Joseph was founded by Mary McKillop, the woman many Australian Roman Catholics hope may some day soon become Australia's first indigenous saint. Born in Melbourne in 1842 of immigrant Scots parents, she began her order under the influence of an extraordinary priest, Father Julian Tenison Woods. A brilliant scholar, Woods was put in charge of developing a proper church school system in South Australia, the first in the country. The Josephites, as Mary's order quickly became known, were the first teachers in the new schools. By 1875, the Josephites were running thirty-five schools in the Catholic diocese of Adelaide.

From the beginning, the new order was different from other, imported, models of the religious life. For a start, the sisters were committed to real poverty. Not only did they teach the poor rather than the middle classes, they also lived extremely simply, depending on school fees (where students could afford to pay any) and on door-to-door begging. They also planned a different kind of organization. Spreading quickly throughout Australia, the order wanted a national identity, free of control of diocesan bishops. They gained their complete independence in 1888, when Pope Leo XIII declared the sisterhood a canonical congregation, and therefore free of diocesan controls.

The sisters' aim of independence was scarcely popular with either Australian bishops or the priests in whose parishes they ran their schools. They faced many crises. Mary's courage and determination alone ensured the survival of her order through its turbulent early years in the face of such fierce resistance from church leaders. By the time of her death in 1909 though, it stood firm, highly regarded for its teaching ministry around the country.

Best known of the orders that set up exclusively male Catholic schools in this country are the Christian Brothers. Brothers from Ireland were encouraged to come to Melbourne in the late 1860s, and soon moved into other states as well. Like the Josephites, they set up a system of schools for the poor. Much of the money to establish the schools came from door-to-door begging. Poor Catholics gave generously, as did many Protestants of goodwill. The early brothers worked hard for long hours, often teaching huge classes in basic buildings with few facilities. Many of them paid for it with their health.

Their achievements were considerable. The sons of poor working-class Roman Catholic families gained the educational qualifications that admitted them to secure employment in business and government. So the way was paved for the transformation of the large Catholic Irish sub-culture from poverty to respectability and influence, effected over only a few generations.

This had been the aim of the Catholic bishops of Australia (and New Zealand) at their first plenary council in 1885. At that meeting, they set the agenda for the church in the antipodes. The first priority, they declared, was the parish school. In every new parish, a school was to be built first and used for Sunday mass until the church could be built. The bishops realized that education was the key to the future for the poor Irish immigrant families that made up the bulk of their church. That made it the key to Catholic influence in the life of the nation in the broadest sense. Their decision was taken up literally, thus ensuring that the parish school became dominant in Catholic life and work.

Catholic education, whether under the various sisterhoods or the Christian Brothers, quickly developed a powerfully distinctive ethos in Australia. It left its mark in various ways on generations of children, so much so that it has been the subject of a proliferation of written works in recent years. Plays, novels and biographies chart the influence of the people and practices associated with this schooling system. A number of Australia's leading literary artists — most of them now lapsed Catholics — have found these childhood experiences rich food for reflection.

Free, compulsory and secular

The Catholic church's record on education in Australia has been good. But, quite deliberately, it established a separatist system. The great failure that must be laid at the door of the mainstream churches in Australia is their failure to support a non-denominational system of Christian schools. They had a number of opportunities to do so, provided by governments largely sympathetic to the claims of the Christian church. However, their complete inability to co-operate left future generations the legacy of a totally secular education.

Faraday state school, Victoria, 1900 (Coo-ee Picture Library).

In the first half of the nineteenth century, there had been various attempts to establish workable school systems. They usually foundered on the rock of Protestant-Roman Catholic antagonism. The compromise was a dual system of state and denominational schools, the latter receiving funds from the various colonial governments. Often, however, church-run schools were less than satisfactory, and as the population grew and expanded into more and more parts of Australia, they were increasingly unable to meet the needs of the situation.

The leading liberal-minded politicians who sought the creation of a state system of schools fully intended to include non-sectarian religious teaching in the curriculum. The Anglican hierarchy and the Roman Catholics were fierce in their opposition to a single system, however. The Roman Catholic Church, with its strong Irish and therefore anti-establishment mentality, was determined to maintain its separateness. But majority Protestant opinion opposed state-aided denominational schools, at least partly because the Roman Catholic Church was making maximum use of the government benefits. Many other Christians were opposed to any kind of state aid for the churches, on the basis that churches should value real independence and look after themselves.

The opposition of the Anglicans and Catholics, their refusal to compromise and the bitterness of their stand, ensured the end of any hopes of integrated general religious teaching in the new free and compulsory state school systems. The very dogmatism of this opposition was anathema to the liberal spirit of the age, which was not anti-religion in general. If the churches could not agree on the form of religious education, the only alternative was for the systems to be "secular". So between 1872 and 1895, all the states ended government funding to church schools entirely, and switched their available money into providing a comprehensive system of "free, compulsory and secular" education, available for all children.

Long before this, the Protestant denominations had virtually bowed out of providing anything like a system of schools. Their schools that survived had no choice but to charge increasingly high fees to cover costs, virtually ensuring that Protestant schooling became the preserve of the economic elite and of those prepared to make substantial financial sacrifices to pay the fees. The Protestants had no armies of unpaid religious to staff their schools! Only in the last few decades has a wider variety of non-government non-Catholic religious schooling become available in some parts of Australia, with the introduction of low-fee Christian community schools and colleges. But they became possible only because the federal government returned a form of state aid to non-government schools in 1963, an astute vote-catching exercise in response to widespread Catholic concern over schooling. Since then, there has been a growing community demand for government funding of non-government schools.

Education today

The end result of the failures of the last century is that religion in Australia's state schools today is largely an "optional extra". By law, a brief period of time must be allocated for religious instruction in primary (junior) schools, but students only attend with parental consent. Outsiders, usually volunteers, trained and nominated by the major religious bodies, provide the lessons. In some states, such as Victoria and Western Australia, an "agreed syllabus" is taught to all children in a programme co-ordinated by an ecumenical council. In other states, the system is an ad hoc one, in which clergy or other representatives of the local churches teach individual curricula. In post-primary (secondary) schools, there is a growing acceptance of school chaplains, appointed by school, church and community together, and usually paid by the latter two bodies.

The nineteenth-century sectarian strife that ensured a secular schooling system also ensured that Australia's first universities were obstinately secular as well. The University of Melbourne, founded in 1853, was expressly forbidden by its statutes to confer degrees in divinity. Instead, the churches were granted land next door to the university, on which they built their own theological colleges. Overt sectarian rivalry at the turn of the century thwarted a golden opportunity to reverse the original statute, when a royal commission suggested that the university should offer a faculty of theology. Again, it was the churches' failure to co-operate which saw the door slam shut once again.

Consequently, the major Protestant churches established the Melbourne College of Divinity, an institution founded by act of parliament in 1910. An examining body, it confers degrees for which students are prepared in the theological colleges. These include students working within the United Faculty of Theology, a recently-established joint enterprise of the Anglican, Uniting and Jesuit theological colleges. Similar associations have been established in other states. It was only in 1972 that the Roman Catholic Church joined the Melbourne College of Divinity, thus confirming it as a highly significant ecumenical institution.

If institutional religion was barred from Australia's first major universities, religion itself could not be. In 1886 the body that was to become the Australian Student Christian Movement was born at an interstate convention organized by the Melbourne University Christian Alliance. Like the SCM in other countries, this interdenominational body would become a seedbed of ecumenism in Australia in the following century. Evangelical unions, Christian fellowships and denominational and ecumenical chaplaincies have also been significant in Australian tertiary education.

Depression and decline

By the turn of the century, the churches' golden age — most evident in Victoria and South Australia rather than the more hedonistic New South Wales — was on the wane. So was the post-gold prosperity of the colonies. Bank crashes and depression, felt most deeply in Victoria, led to high unemployment and consequent increased mobility as families followed available work. The crashes devastated some of the churches' most respectable and generous members. Some poorer members loosened their connections in the dislocations of the time. Australia's first major industrial upheavals resulted in crippling strikes, particularly the shearers' and maritime strikes of 1890 and the Broken Hill (mining) strike of 1892. Suddenly the days of seemingly endless growth and prosperity were over.

The abrupt end of what had seemed to be the ever-ascending progress of Christian society left Protestantism somewhat confused. Many of its leaders at the turn of the century bewailed the vice and profanity they saw all around them, and were deeply pessimistic for the future of Australia. The population might still be officially Christian (census figures in New South Wales revealed that 97 percent of people called themselves Christian between 1871 and 1921) but fewer people were attending church. Most of them were middle class. The working classes were still largely neglected.

In this period of high unemployment, life for many working-class people was appalling. Like the Britain so many hopeful immigrants had left, Australia too had slums, and bad working conditions with low rates of pay and long hours of work. Children and women had to work to earn a basic family living in some cases. Many in Sydney's poor inner suburbs drank heavily to ease their plight, and many religious people believed that it was moral reform, rather than social reform, that was necessary.

However, some vigorous and innovative social welfare programmes were begun to meet the needs of the time. This was the age when the central Methodist missions began their pioneering work in the seamy inner areas of Sydney and Melbourne. They worked hard to meet the many individual needs which came their way, but also campaigned for the social change that would alleviate the problems. Many social justice issues have been tackled from the missions since the turn of the century, from slum clearance and housing programmes to alcoholic rehabilitation, working conditions and wage levels. Lifeline, the international telephone counselling service, originated in the Sydney Central Methodist Mission in 1963.

The Salvation Army's social relief ministry had its beginnings in Melbourne in the last decades of the nineteenth century. Major James Barker opened a hostel for released prisoners in 1883, just three years after the Army first came to Australia. Institutions for unmarried mothers, the homeless, alcoholics, old people and children followed. Today the Salvation Army enjoys a high reputation in Australia, where memories of its outstanding work among the armed forces during the two world wars remain vivid.

But at the turn of the century, the overwhelming official concern of the Protestant churches lay in moral reform. A morally upright, Christian Australia would be a society without social evils. So during the late nineteenth and early twentieth centuries, the major concern of the Protestant churches was the moral health of society. At its centre lay home and family, proclaimed to be the heart of the nation, and therefore to be protected from all possible evils.

Temperance

Major target of the moral reformers was alcohol. It was the obvious starting point in a society where alcohol had been heavily consumed since the days when rum was the settlement's currency. Temperance became the catch-cry, though in fact the word quickly came to mean total abstinence rather than moderation. The Methodist church was the strongest advocate of "temperance", and so the push for severe limitation on the sale and consumption of alcohol was strongest in states where Methodism was strongest, notably Victoria and South Australia. The local hotel — "pub" — became the target of the abstainers, and many attempts were made to legislate them out of existence by coalitions of church leaders and politicians. Some saw this as a direct attack on the working classes, for whom pubs were a social centre. Drinking at home or in clubs, as the middle classes did, was never under such a sustained level of attack. But then, drink was fervently believed to be the curse of the working classes, who could ill afford either alcohol or its after-effects. Pubs were male enclaves which kept men away from their wives and families, thus weakening the moral influence of "the home".

The most notorious method of control was six o'clock closing. Until the first world war, pubs had remained open virtually all day and the entire evening, not closing until 11.30 p.m. During the war, the states of Victoria, New South Wales, South Australia and Tasmania enforced six o'clock closing as a patriotic measure. In some ill-defined way, limited drinking, it was believed, would strengthen the battle against the Kaiser. It was intended to be a temporary measure, but the power of the temperance unions and their mainline church backers ensured that it remained in force until the late 1960s.

Its main legacy was a grotesque social practice known as the six o'clock swill. Working men raced to the pub as their working day ended. In bare, comfortless bars they endeavoured to drink as much liquor — mainly beer — as quickly as they could in the brief half-hour they had at their disposal. Coupled with the well-entrenched Australian custom of "shouting" — each man in a group must buy a round of drinks for everyone else in any one drinking session — it ensured that prodigious quantities of alcohol were consumed quickly. Many men reeled drunkenly home each night after the pub doors closed. Coalitions of Protestant churches tried to prevent the repeal of early closing legislation until the bitter end. In Sydney they even marched on parliament, but eventually drinking hours became more leisurely. Pubs have, in the main, become more civilized places as a consequence, providing comfortable bars and added attractions such as music and bistro meals. They are no longer exclusively male preserves.

Next on the reformers' list was gambling. Many Australians are inveterate gamblers. Perhaps the vagaries of our climate have instilled the instinct, as every decision to plant or harvest or stock land is, in a very real sense, a gamble. There is a saying that Australians would bet on two flies crawling up a wall! The Protestant churches, deploring the vast amounts of money wasted on gambling on horse races in particular, strongly opposed all attempts to legalize off-course betting. Despite their efforts, including many sermons on the subject, illegal off-course betting remained a fact of Australian life, with a local bookmaker often operating out of the local pub.

Wowsers

Much of the churches' opposition to alcohol and gambling was justified. Both were serious problems. Unfortunately, such opposition went hand in hand with a prudish condemnation of many forms of public amusement. Methodists forbad dancing, and other churches frowned on it earlier this century. There was heated debate about billiards, the theatre, even cricket. The great symbol of this level of moral seriousness was the struggle to keep Sunday a "holy" day. Some clergy went so far as to maintain that a pure sabbath lay at the heart of the strength of the British empire.

The Sabbatarians had their greatest victory in Melbourne. This stronghold of stern Protestantism proudly upheld the dullest and quietest Sunday in Australia until only a few decades ago. Public transport was provided only to ferry people to and from church, Sunday newspapers were banned lest paper boys disturb worship with their sales pitch, and there were long and heated arguments before the public library and the state art gallery were opened on Sundays. It took until the 1960s before sport and films on Sundays became legal. It was only in 1989 that the major newspaper proprietors began to publish Sunday editions, exactly one hundred years after Sunday newspapers were banned by parliament.

Even swimwear has been a source of controversy for the churches. Today the scantiest of swimwear is commonplace on Australian beaches, the great summer playground for Australians of all ages. There are also a few beaches set aside for nude bathing. Clergy no longer seem concerned at this state of affairs, but not so their predecessors, who fought hard against daylight bathing, then mixed bathing, and finally, "immodest" bathing attire.

Many who fought these moral battles did so for praiseworthy motives. But too often the narrow prudery and carping "killjoy" attitudes of a minority earned them the name of "wowsers", a distinctive Australian tag of abuse. Unfortunately, the name was often attached to the churches in general. The aura of stern moralism and middle-class respectability they promoted has clung to all the churches, a legacy that has proved to be very tenacious.

Women and family

Much of the moral reform debate of the early twentieth century was part of the Protestant churches' adulation of family and motherhood at this time. Ironically, it led to their support for votes for women. Women, the reformers believed, would automatically cast their vote in favour of any measure that would improve family life. Therefore women could be relied on to support legislation against alcohol, gambling and other social evils. The Women's Christian Temperance Union in particular promoted the vote for women for these very reasons. Australia had only a small organized women's movement at this time. In fact, the connection with the temperance movement may well have disadvantaged the push for votes for women. But a variety of other political factions had high hopes that women's votes would be to their advantage, and so it was that women gained this right in Australia many years before their counterparts in Great Britain and the United States. The first state to extend the vote to women was South Australia in 1894. The other states followed over the next fourteen years, with Victoria the last in 1908. They had gained the right to vote in federal elections in 1902, a year after the formation of the Australian common-wealth.

Federation

In the latter half of the nineteenth century, the six indepen-dent colonies had to face the question of federation. The colonial rivalries were still powerful, but the linking of the major cities and towns by rail and telegraph had minimized the old tyranny of distance between them. There was a growing sense of nationalism, fostered in particular by the school of poets and writers who found ready publication in the Sydney-based magazine, *The Bulletin*. Economic interests, however, were probably the strongest impetus to federation as farmers and businessmen increasingly recognized that they needed Australia-wide, rather than state-wide, markets for their goods. The protectionist tariffs imposed by the individual states were severely limiting.

After several attempts, a federal constitution finally came into

The Parliament House complex, Canberra

force on 1 January 1901. The constitution left the states a high degree of autonomy in several areas such as health, education and transport. The commonwealth government would control international relations, tariff protection, defence, post and tele-graph services, taxation and other areas which required a national approach. Canberra, an artificial national capital, was created to overcome the intense rivalry between the two largest cities, Sydney and Melbourne.

The Australian legend

What kind of society was Australia as it celebrated its new, independent nationhood at the turn of the century? It was, a little more that 100 years after white settlement, beginning to feel a sense of Australian patriotism. The service of king and empire still stirred Australian hearts, which continued to be proud of the British heritage. The colonial cringe would last well into the second half of the new century, and the nostalgia for the old world would cling to many of the second- and third-generation immigrants. But a pride and love of native land was emerging powerfully.

Though Australia was already highly urbanized, the typical Australian remained the bushman. Male gender for the typical Aussie was assumed; the "Australian legend" reflected the dominance of the masculine in Australian society. The legendary Australian was a tough, laconic character who seldom gave way to emotion, let alone spiritu-ality. The important relationships in his life were with his mates, not his wife and family. His humour was dry, and his pleasures few — drinking with his mates, a quiet smoke, a flutter (gamble) on the horses. He despised the wowsers who wanted to take away these pleasures, and the clergy who seemed, by and large, less than manly. The bushman doffed his hat to no man — this was the land of equality — and prized his independence. He despised artistic and intellectual pursuits, had no time for "tall poppies" (outstandingly able people) and had little respect for education. At best suspi-cious of police and other authority figures, he obeyed the law and paid his taxes, but grudgingly.

This was the Australian image romanticized by Henry Law-son, "Banjo" Patterson and other late nineteenth-century writers made famous by *The Bulletin*. Few Australians then or now conformed to all its characteristics, but the image remains a powerful one. Urban working- and middle-class Australians, living quietly in comfortable suburbia, still like to identify with the bushman. He remains an attractive figure who is essentially Australian in ways that the city executive, the professional man, the shop-keeper can never be. Certainly no woman, or person male or female from anything other than a white British background, can hope to be "Australian" in the same way.

Racism

The most unattractive features of the legendary Aussie are his powerfully negative attitudes to women and even more strident racism. In the late nineteenth century, as the legend was popularized by *The Bulletin* writers, Australia was in the grip of a particularly ugly racism. One legacy of the gold rushes was a hatred of the Chinese and fear of the perceived threat the "yellow peril" posed for white Anglo-Celtic purity. As the Chinese gold miners became market gardeners, tradesmen and farm workers, fear that they were depriving white people of work lay behind the formation of anti-Chinese leagues, particularly in Victoria and New South Wales.

Specific industrial problems over Chinese labour, such as the one that caused the seamen's strike of 1878-79, only fuelled the fears. Further industrial confrontation and growing levels of unemployment prompted even more anti-Chinese hatred, and led to the almost total prohibition of Chinese immigration in all colonies by the last decade of the nineteenth century.

So it was that "white Australia" was the policy of each of the three parties which contested the first federal parliamentary elections. Consequently, the Immigration Restriction Act, which endorsed all the restrictions on coloured races of the separate colonies, was introduced in the first session of the new parliament. Race homogeneity was the proclaimed ideal. Alfred Deakin, soon to become Australia's second prime minister, claimed that all Australians wanted the new nation "to be one people and remain one people without the admixture of other races". Few doubted that coloured people were inferior to white people, so it was a white, Anglo-Celtic society that most Australians sought as the colonies became one nation. Some presented this case in lofty, nationalistic terms. Others, in particular many writers in *The Bulletin*, were guilty of the ugliest forms of naked racist hatred.

Overt discrimination against people of other races, including Australia's own indigenous population, would continue well into the second half of the twentieth century, ensuring that the benefits of the new nation belonged largely to white people. As these policies were formulated, refined and enacted at the turn of the century, few if any church leaders spoke up against them. Many in fact endorsed them. As with the treatment of the Aborigines earlier, the implicit assumption was that white, preferably British, civilization went hand in hand with Christianity.

A Christian nation?

As the new commonwealth of Australia moved into the twentieth century, how far could it be called a Christian nation? Census statistics of the time reveal that 97 percent of the population called themselves Christians. The federal constitution briefly acknowledged God, but ensured the separation of church and state by forbidding federal parliament to establish any religion, or prohibit any religion. The school system and the universities were thoroughly secular. The post-gold rush heyday for the churches might be over, but in every town and suburb church services were still relatively well-attended. The churches retained their virtual monopoly on marriage and death, and many people continued to respect the clergy.

In the coming century, however, the churches would pay the price of the failures of the nineteenth century. The failures — to attract or serve the needs of the working classes, to adapt a European style of ministry to a vastly different climate and terrain, to incarnate Christian theology in Australian experience, to overcome the hostilities and prejudices of the old world — would all exact a heavy penalty.

3. Becoming a Nation

The newly formed commonwealth of Australia moved into the twentieth century determined to protect the interests of its tiny white population. Immigration restrictions effectively kept out the vast Asian numbers so close to Australia's borders, and so fearfully regarded since the days of the gold rushes. Nor was there any threat closer to home. The indigenous Aborigines were rapidly declining, their ancient culture and spirituality only surviving perilously in a few parts of the country where distance prevented total annihilation. The days of indiscriminate and unchallenged slaughter were over, but disease, dispossession, exploitation and despair continued to take a terrible toll.

In the nineteenth century, most whites, including some church leaders, had assumed that the imminent extinction of the race was inevitable, and even claimed theological justification for it. However, some far-sighted and compassionate people, mostly missionaries, stood between the Aborigines and their complete destruction. By modern lights, even these men and women were misguided in many respects. Too often they insisted on the elimination of traditional ways, believing them to be incompatible with Christianity, which was naturally equated in their minds with Europeanization. But they ensured that a remnant of the race survived into the twentieth century. The

An early 20th century Aboriginal mission, Queensland. Aboriginal children placed in such institutions were sometimes harshly treated. Many lost contact with their families and traditional life-styles (Coo-ee Picture Library).

Christian missions' major historical achievement was as places of survival, historian Dr John Harris has recently pointed out.

Not that the twentieth century brought any different future for Australia's Aborigines. Aboriginal affairs remained the preserve of state governments despite federation, until the late 1960s. In the name of "protecting" the last members of the dying race, Aboriginal reserves were established around the country. Many of them were originally Christian missions, taken into secular control. Aboriginal people were forced to live detribalized, regimented lives in an often oppressive and dehumanizing atmosphere. The democratic freedoms white Australians enjoyed, and so proudly defended in world wars, were denied them. Part-Aboriginal children came under cruel regulations designed to assimilate them into white society. It has been estimated that 5,600 children were forcibly taken from their parents in New South Wales alone between 1900 and 1969. The nationwide total would be far higher. Usually removed by police without warning, the children were placed in institutions where the use of their own language was often forbidden, as was their traditional life-style. All family contact was often lost for ever. Many of these institutions were harsh and joyless places where Aborigines were treated with contempt, and trained once more to be servants and labourers. There were, of course, the exceptions; some institutions were kindly places run by compassionate Christians or humanists.

Nevertheless, the Christian churches by and large either ignored or condoned this large-scale cultural genocide in their midst. Few church leaders spoke up for the stolen generations. Most white Australians, certainly in the major cities, knew little or nothing about it. In many respects, it was a well-kept secret, but only because few cared enough to ask any questions. Only in recent years, as Aborigines have written and spoken about their past, has the tragic story become more widely known. Though the most devastating discriminatory policies ended when the commonwealth government gained a role in Aboriginal affairs in 1969, the date from which indigenous Australians were at last officially recognized as Australians, the deeply traumatic repercussions could not so easily be eliminated. The recent abnormally high suicide rates of Aborigines in police custody, and the deep-rooted fear and hatred many Aborigines feel for police, have been linked to these earlier policies.

Unity moves

In the first decade of the new century, the Christian churches were themselves touched by the spirit of federalism. The three main strands of Methodism in Australia — the Wesleyans, the Primitive Methodists and Bible Christians — became the Methodist Conference of Australia in 1902. But wider moves for a more comprehensive reunion of the Protestant churches were in hand. The national Presbyterian General Assembly, itself a recently federated body, had in 1901 invited other Protestant churches to consider union. The Methodists and the Congregationalists were the obvious partners, and some progress was made.

For a while an even wider union seemed possible. There were negotiations for a time with both the Baptists and the Anglicans. But by 1912, both had withdrawn, and union discussions were once more limited to Presbyterians, Methodists and Congregationalists. On a number of occasions they came very close to agreement, but increasing opposition within Presbyterianism spelt doom. By 1922, the union proposals were abandoned when it became clear that the issue could split the Presbyterian Church. In many ways, the process was a precursor of the eventual union of the same three churches in 1977, at which time the feared split in the Presbyterian Church sadly became a reality.

A separate people

But if the Protestants were experimenting with union, Roman Catholics were still in many respects a separate people. The consuming passion to establish their own schooling system had created a wide Catholic cultural network. Even non-church-going Catholics were drawn into the many activities which supported the schools, and thus became part of Catholic social, sporting and political organizations. St Patrick's Day become a mammoth celebration of Irish Catholicism, with its sporting events and a big street march through Melbourne. The crusade against mixed marriages led by the Catholic bishops from the 1860s on ensured a high level of Catholic identity and cohesion, though at the expense of family division and personal anguish.

Australia had experienced high levels of anti-Catholic feeling in the latter half of the nineteenth century. The attempted assassination by an Irishman of Australia's first royal visitor in 1868, Queen Victoria's son Prince Alfred, had caused an outbreak of anti-Irish sentiment. Fiercely Protestant bodies such as the Loyal Orange Institution enjoyed spectacular growth in the following years. Employers began to specify "Protestants only" in job advertisements. Sectarian bitterness remained an unpleasant reality of Australian life in the first decades of the twentieth century.

The churches and party politics

Australia's party political system owes its origins to this crucial period, and so for most of this century has inevitably reflected some of that sectarian separate development. In particular, the Labor Party was affected. Today the Labor Party is a democratic socialist party with broad support, but it began as a party to represent the interests of the working classes, as its name reveals. With Catholics comprising a significant majority of the working classes, it was the obvious party with which they should align.

Ironically, the earliest religious influences on the Labor Party had in fact come from Protestants. In the latter years of the nineteenth century, Protestant individuals, lay people, had had an important impact on the development of the Labor movement, imparting to it a moral earnestness which survived up to very recent times. But Protestant middle-class and employer interests were most obviously represented by the forerunners of what are now the Liberal and National Parties, and so Protestant political influence, both lay and hierarchical, was soon strongest there. Catholics, both working and middle-class, however, gave their allegiance to Labor. In recent years these clear-cut divisions have largely dissipated. Protestants and Catholics no longer inhabit such markedly separate worlds, class boundaries have become increasingly fluid, and consequently the political parties no longer represent such clearly defined class interests.

The political manifestations of sectarian bitterness became most obvious during the first world war. In 1916 the Australian

Labor government came under pressure from the British government to supply more and more soldiers for the battlefields of Europe. The prime minister, Billy Hughes, proposed to introduce conscription to meet the demand. The Anglican synod in Melbourne supported him wholeheartedly in what they declared to be a "religious war", in which God was using the allies to uphold the moral order. However, not all Australians agreed with this interpretation. There was large-scale grassroots opposition from within the Labor Party, which forced Hughes to take the question to the people in the form of a referendum. Hughes and his supporters were expelled from the Labor Party, and the referendum was fiercely opposed. Both that referendum and a second one the following year were lost. An important factor in their defeat was not merely the party opposition. Incensed by the British defeat of the Easter uprising in Ireland in 1916, Irish Catholic sentiment was implacably opposed to forcing Australian men to fight for the British empire. Daniel Mannix, the controversial Catholic archbishop of Melbourne and a fierce Irish nationalist, led Catholic opposition to conscription. This support for the Labor Party cemented the relationship between the two bodies at the same time as it fuelled the sectarian divide in Australian society.

The Anzac myth

Australia's physical isolation, so often a liability, has protected it from most of the horrors of modern warfare. During the first world war, it was half a world away from the gunfire, and yet that conflict had a profound, even traumatic effect on the young nation. Australian soldiers had gone off to fight for the empire in the past; they served with distinction in the British-Boer War of 1899-1902. But in 1915, they marched off to war as members of an independent fighting force for the first time. The Australian and New Zealand Army Corps (Anzac) were to make their mark in many of the famous battles of the war. No less than sixty-six soldiers would be awarded the British Empire's highest award for valour, the Victoria Cross. Some 330,000 Australians — one quarter of the country's men — went to war in the only entirely volunteer army in action. Sixty thousand were killed and many more wounded, proportionately the highest rate of all the empire armies. The high casualty rate

Some 330,000 Australians — one quarter of the country's men — joined the Australian and New Zealand Army Corps (Anzac) to fight in the first world war; 7,600 Australian soldiers in this entirely volunteer army died in the ill-fated Gallipoli campaign, commemorated each year on Anzac Day 25 April (Coo-ee Picture Library).

is not surprising, however, as Australian troops were regularly used as front-line shock troops. That was their main function in their first major campaign, Gallipoli.

The assault on Gallipoli, on the Dardanelles, was designed by the British general staff to force a passage through to Constantinople. But from the first it was a virtually impossible task, and nothing short of a military disaster. The invading armies — British, French, Australian and New Zealand — had to scale the sheer heights of Gallipoli under relentless fire from the waiting Turkish soldiers. They battled on for eight months, but finally had to withdraw, their objective in tatters.

It had been a costly, terrible defeat. Wave after wave of men were mown down. Australia alone lost 7,600 soldiers, and nearly three times as many were wounded. But the defeat has been turned into a symbol of valour in Australian mythology. The day the ill-fated campaign began — 25 April 1915 — was quickly designated Anzac Day, and soon became the "one day of the year" for Australians. It is on Anzac Day each year that Australia, like New Zealand, remembers its war dead and honours returned veterans in marches and commemorations.

But Anzac Day is more than veterans' day, and much more than just another public holiday. It is a unique national day which vastly transcends in importance even Australia Day, the anniversary of white settlement which is celebrated on 26 January. It is observed more solemnly, indeed more religiously, than Good Friday. Regulations about its observance are stricter than for any other day.

It was the Gallipoli campaign, disastrous as it was, that first enabled Australia to be recognized as an autonomous nation. And not only outsiders saluted the fact that a former cluster of colonies was now an independent sovereign state. Australians themselves began to see themselves as Australians, rather than as Victorians or South Australians or Tasmanians. Federation was internalized at last.

Australians as an individual race — no longer expatriate Englishmen or Irishmen or Scots — were also recognized for the first time. As members of a volunteer army which insisted on a high standard of physical fitness in its recruits, they were usually men of fine physique. They were also a high-spirited lot, who fought hard and played hard and laughed off petty army discipline.

The cheerful bronzed Aussie soldier quickly became a myth — a myth curiously like the earlier bushman myth. The mythical Anzac was a bit of a larrikin, not given to emotion or religion, laconic, cheeky to his superiors, and dry of wit. But most of all he was loyal to his mates. Once more the legendary Australian was the loner male hero of the outdoors. Australian soldiers were quickly termed "diggers", linking them in the popular imagination with the folk heroes of Eureka. Veterans are still often called "old diggers", a term of endearment and respect in the unemotional language of everyday Australia.

The Anzac myth, both of the birth of nationhood and the creation of the digger hero, quickly passed into the fabric of Australian life. It was widely praised and regularly commemorated, and taught in hushed tones to every generation of schoolchildren until the last decade or so. It is perhaps the one symbol that brings a lump to the throat of many average citizens. In a nation given to good-humoured debunking of most "sacred cows", Anzac and Gallipoli are words which summon up deep pride and reverence. Theologians have identified an underlying though rarely acknowledged dependence on the Christian understanding of sacrifice and resurrection beneath the myth's continuing power.

It was bolstered after the war by two initiatives. The first was the formation of the forerunner of the Returned Services League, a singularly successful veterans' organization which has

---

The Women of the West
They left the vine-wreathed cottage and the mansion on the hill,
The houses in the busy streets where life is never still,
The pleasures of the city, and the friends they cherished best:
For love they faced the wilderness — the Women of the West.

The roar, and rush, and fever of the city died away,
And the old-time joys and faces — they were gone for many a day;
In their place the lurching coach-wheel, or the creaking bullock chains,
O'er the everlasting sameness of the never-ending plains.

In the slab-built, zinc-roofed homestead of some lately-taken run,
In the tent beside the bankment of a railway just begun,
In the huts on new selections, in the camps of man's unrest,
On the frontiers of the Nation, live the Women of the West.

The red sun robs their beauty, and, in weariness and pain,
The slow years steal the nameless grace that never comes again;
And there are hours men cannot soothe, and words men cannot say —
The nearest woman's face may be a hundred miles away.

A bush home, c.1890 (Coo-ee Picture Library).

> The wide Bush holds the secrets of their longings and desires,
> When the white stars in reverence light their holy altar-fires,
> And silence, like the touch of God, sinks deep into the breast —
> Perchance He hears and understands the Women of the West.
>
> For them no trumpet sounds the call, no poet plies his arts —
> They only hear the beating of their gallant, loving hearts.
> But they have sung with silent lives the song all songs above —
> The holiness of sacrifice, the dignity of love.
>
> Well have we held our father's creed. No call has passed us by.
> We faced and fought the wilderness, we sent our sons to die.
> And we have hearts to do and dare, and yet, o'er all the rest,
> The hearts that made the Nation were the Women of the West.
>
> *G. Essex Evans, 1863-1909*

championed conservative political policies. It was the self-appointed caretaker of the legend, as well as of the white, God-king-and-country society it believed its members had gone to war to fight for. RSL clubs, found in every town of any size, provide a meeting place for old diggers where they can happily relive past glories of what was perhaps the most significant time of their lives. In quasi-religious rituals, the war dead are regularly remembered at club meetings. When old diggers die, an RSL ritual is a frequent addition to the funeral service. So the RSL has become a form of church-going for many Australians who have long since abandoned the more conventional kind.

The second post-war initiative was the establishment of war memorials. Every little settlement up and down the country has a statue of a strong young digger in his distinctive slouch hat, or a war memorial community hall, or at the very least an honour board in some public location. Sydney, Melbourne and Canberra all have large and imposing war memorials which take the form of national shrines of remembrance. They are conceived and built in the form of Greek tombs or temples, set in carefully trimmed and symmetrical grounds. Like their classical counterparts, they are places set apart. In their halls of memory, the fallen soldiers are transformed into classical heroes. There is scarcely a Christian or even a theist symbol to be found in these monuments.

The shrines are the heart of Anzac Day commemorations, which are almost always "religious" rather than Christian. Half-mast flags, bugles, wreaths, and eternal flames are the potent symbols on these occasions and state and RSL leaders are more important than clergy. It is sobering that the most solemn, mystical and popular religious event of the Australian calendar should be so manifestly non-Christian in a country which until very recently was more than 90 percent Christian. The churches, however, have not seemed overly concerned by their exclusion. Perhaps the myth has had significant meaning for too many church leaders personally for it to be seriously questioned.

Taming the bush

The churches' activities were not confined to moralistic outrage, the creation of welfare organizations and sectarian politicking in the first half of the twentieth century. At last, in a variety of ways, they began to come to terms with the realities of Australian distances. They had learnt to their cost that the parish system was not suited to the sparsely populated areas of inland Australia. Long distances kept clergy and people apart, and there were too few people to support parish clergy financially anyway. Loneliness had been the ultimate downfall of many ministers in the bush.

One Anglican solution to the problem was the bush brotherhoods, founded by Bishop Nathaniel Dawes of Rockhampton when he established the Brotherhood of St Andrew at Longreach, Queensland, in 1897 with English volunteers.

A few years later, the rector of the far western New South Wales town of Dubbo invited two young English priests to join him, with the intention of establishing another brotherhood, the Brotherhood of the Good Shepherd. Its members would agree to live in poverty, chastity and obedience for five years. The ideal was that the brothers would work in pairs, coming back at regular intervals to headquarters for rest and recreation. Loneliness would thus be overcome, while the commitment not to marry would leave the brothers free from family concerns. The subsistence payment would hopefully make the whole operation financially viable.

Freddie Campion and Charles Matthews, the first Good Shepherd brothers, began their bush ministry in blistering heat and severe drought conditions. They held church services in crude church buildings, but also in hotel bars, in farm sheds, and in the open air. They married, baptized and buried, and struggled to overcome the long years of neglect when bush people had not seen a parson for years at a time. They vowed to stop at every dwelling they passed, and to speak to everyone they met on the track. The result was that they and their immediate successors wore themselves out with endless travelling and endless work.

Eventually ten brotherhoods were established in all, in New South Wales, Queensland, South Australia and Western Australia. The Brotherhoods of the Good Shepherd, St Barnabas (Townsville, Queensland) and St Paul (Charleville, Queensland) lasted the longest. Today, the Brotherhood of the Good Shepherd still survives as an incorporated body, distributing the income from investments to church projects across the outback. One recent recipient has been an Aboriginal ministry, based in the old Brotherhood House in Dubbo.

The bush brotherhoods, however, had not escaped controversy during their developmental period. The fact that they were Anglo-Catholic in origin and style of ministry had met with some hostility from Sydney Evangelicals in particular. So in 1919 a separate form of Anglican ministry in the outback — the Bush Church Aid Society — was established. This society, which is still in existence, quickly provided clergy for outback areas. A correspondence Sunday school soon followed, as well as travelling mission vans and, in 1928, a mission plane in the Wilcannia region.

But the society did not depend solely on clergy for its mission. Women undertook much of its work in an age when there was little opportunity for them to serve in the city churches. Some were hostel sisters, caring for children accommodated in a series of hostels in country centres. These allowed children from remote areas to receive an education. Deaconesses toured inland areas, bringing Christian worship and education to isolated families. Nurses ran the hospitals and clinics set up by the society.

Some years before the advent of BCA, however, the most comprehensive and famous of the Christian outback missions had begun. John Flynn, a Victorian-born Presbyterian minister, was fired with compassion for the needs of the white people scattered across the vast outback. They lived cut off from the most basic services that their city cousins took for granted. Not only clergy but doctors were few and far between. Long and hair-raising journeys on rough bush tracks were the only link with the outside world.

In 1909, Flynn had taken part in a shearers' mission in inland Victoria, and had realized how hard life was for many. He heard of bushmen who were forced to bury a dead mate without benefit of clergy. One of the impromptu undertakers told him that they had had no Bible, no hymn book, with which to conduct a service, and so ended up standing around the grave, singing "Auld Lang Syne"! A man of imagination as well as of immense energy and determination, Flynn set to work to prepare a "Bushman's Companion". This little pocketbook, published in its thousands and distributed free of charge, contained a funeral service for just such occasions. As well, it included Bible selections, prayers and hymns, and a host of practical information such as notes on first aid.

By 1912, Flynn had conducted a wide-ranging survey of the needs of the outback for the Presbyterian Church. The result was the foundation of the Australian Inland Mission, which would eventually revolutionize the quality of life in the outback. Over the years, it established a string of hospitals, old timers' (retirement) homes, children's holiday centres, and many other services. The AIM's "patrol padres" were outback clergy who, like their brothers in the Anglican Church's services, travelled long distances and worked long hours to bring the ministry of word and sacrament to isolated people.

But Flynn's two most imaginative schemes were to make his name a household word around Australia and, more importantly, to cast what he called "a mantle of safety" over the outback. Flynn was most concerned about the severe limitations on health services in the inland of the continent. Even with motorized transport, the terrible roads across long distances could make the summoning of medical help a time-consuming

The isolation of people living on outback cattle stations — whose nearest neighbours may live hundreds of kilometres away — was greatly alleviated with the advent of pedal wireless, a flying doctor service, and a "school of the air" (Coo-ee Picture Library).

and hazardous business. Bush people could all tell harrowing stories of needless deaths from illness and accident because there was no fast means of getting assistance. This meant that women and children were loath to live in the bush, leaving the frontier to lonely single males and a few brave families.

Flynn was convinced that the answer lay in two recent modern inventions, the aeroplane and wireless communication. But they were both new and untested, and many dismissed the possibility out of hand. Flynn was nothing if not persistent, and determined that his dream would not die. By the late 1920s, after years of badgering politicians and businessmen, and of encouraging inventors, the first flying-doctor service and a simple, reliable wireless system, were inaugurated. The wireless, pedal-powered in its early days, was cheap enough to become a household necessity across the bush; portable, it could accompany the patrol padres or stockmen alike into the lonely wilderness. So the bush was given a voice, and help could be summoned immediately in time of trouble. Doctors could be dispatched by air hundreds of miles to sick and injured people, and patients easily transported to hospital where necessary.

Together, the two innovations tamed the Australian outback. In time, the flying-doctor service would cover most of the continent. The wireless service brought more than safety, however. It brought community, and conquered the terrible loneliness of the outback. Isolated families could keep in daily touch with each other, and with the wider world. Radio broadcasts became available, along with telegram and other communication services. Eventually the "school of the air", which brings primary-level education to youngsters on remote properties, was developed.

Flynn's motto, "For Christ and the Continent", lives on as the motto of Frontier Services, the outback mission arm of the Uniting Church in Australia. It combines the work of the (Presbyterian) AIM, and of the inland operations of the Methodist and Congregational churches, joined together when the Uniting Church was formed. Today the Royal Flying Doctor Service is an independent charitable body, funded by governments and donations, but it retains close links with Frontier Services. It now covers two-thirds of Australia from thirteen bases with thirty-four aircraft, treating 105,000 patients a year.

At war again

If the great war marked the beginning of Australia's nation-hood, the second world war saw a massive change in Australia's fundamental perception of its place in the world. Until the 1939-45 war, Australia's foreign policy was still firmly wedded to that of Great Britain. In many respects, the colonial ties were as strong as ever. But all that was to change.

Of Australia's population of seven million, almost one million joined the armed forces during the second world war. More than 33,000 died on active service, including 7,964 who died as prisoners of war of the Japanese. The survivors of the death camps, who returned home little more than walking skeletons, brought with them the makings of another legend of Australians at war. Amazing stories of courage, resourcefulness, kindness and above all mateship amidst the extreme privation and terrible illnesses the prisoners of war had suffered, illumined a gentler version of the Anzac warrior. Here was the digger, half-starved and disabled with dysentery instead of the bronzed demi-god of Gallipoli, nursing a dying mate with all the tender love of a Florence Nightingale. Some of the survivors would claim that they experienced more of the love of God in Changi prison camp or on the slave labour teams of the Burma railway than at any other time of their lives.

This war came much closer to home than the great war. On 19 February 1942, without prior warning, Japanese planes bombed the northern capital of Darwin, sinking ships and killing 243 civilians. It was the first of many such raids on the northern coast over the following twenty months. In May 1942, Japanese midget submarines penetrated Sydney harbour, sinking a depot ship and firing shells into some of Sydney's most prestigious suburbs. Although Australia's civilian losses were negligible compared to those of the ravaged cities of Europe, at the time they seemed a foretaste of worse to come. The Japanese threat was real, and frightening. Trenches for civil defence were built in parks and playgrounds across suburban Australia; prominent landmarks were disguised and windows blacked-out in preparation for either large-scale air-raids or actual invasion. In the event, neither happened.

It was in the context of the Japanese threat that Australia's federal government made its decisive shift of alignment to the

United States of America. At the end of 1941, when the fall of the British base of Singapore made it clear that Britain could no longer protect Australia, prime minister John Curtin told Australians: "Without any inhibitions of any kind, I make it quite clear that Australia looks to America, free of any pangs as to our traditional links or kinship with the United Kingdom." So the ground was cleared for the future Anzus defence treaty, which would link Australia and New Zealand with the military power of the United States. It would also lead to Australia's involvement in two of America's wars — Korea and Vietnam.

So while the first world war created a recognizable nation of Australia, it was the second world war which finally cut the umbilical cord with England. Australia recognized that its destiny was not with the old world of Europe, but with the new world represented by America. Many would still feel powerful sentimental ties with Great Britain, as the continuing allegiance to the British monarchy shows. But the shift of political and military allegiance effectively liberated Australia from its colonial past, setting it free for its development into an exciting, multicultural society in the post-war period.

A different kind of cultural dependence has developed, however. The new alliance meant that American culture and lifestyle had an ever-increasing influence on Australia, particularly after television was introduced in 1956. From its beginnings, Australian television has been overwhelmingly American in both style and content, leading to the consistent and pervasive Americanization of Australian society.

A common voice

The churches, instead of being divided by war as they had been in 1914-18, were united this time in a common enterprise. Protestants and Catholics alike combined in their opposition to Hitler and the Japanese. Even conscription, this time introduced with little demur, could not divide them from each other or national policy. Though the rhetoric of the first world war was no longer current, most Christians accepted that this time they were indeed fighting a moral war against the horrors of fascism.

So the churches increasingly recognized the need to have a united Christian voice in Australia, particularly for the post-war reconstruction period. Though the attempt at reunion by the Presbyterian, Methodist and Congregational Churches had failed during the 1920s, that was the decade which nevertheless saw the development of other unity moves. In 1922, at the instigation of the Anglican primate, Archbishop John Wright of Sydney, a conference of the main Protestant churches was called together. They formed the Joint Australian Council of the Churches Contemplating Reunion, which met until the 1930s. However, Anglican intransigence over episcopacy and episcopal ordination brought the venture to an end.

The New South Wales Council of Churches was formed in 1925, and a National Missionary Council of Australia in 1926, which included representatives not only of Protestant churches but also of bodies such as the Australian Student Christian Movement. Over the years, the National Missionary Council would prove to be a forward-thinking and influential body, an early advocate of citizenship and land rights for Aboriginal Australians.

By 1934, the Victorian regional committee of the Faith and Order movement had been formed, including in its number representatives of the small Baptist, Lutheran, Greek and Syrian Orthodox Churches as well as the Society of Friends, the Anglicans, Presbyterians, Methodists and Congregationalists by the outbreak of war. By 1940, it had become the regional committee for the World Council of Churches, itself still in the process of formation. By the end of the war, regional committees had also been formed in New South Wales, Western Australia, Tasmania and the Australian Capital Territory, paving the way for the formation of the national body in 1946. This, the World Council of Churches (Australian section), later became the Australian Council of Churches which today has thirteen member churches.

The role of women

Sixty-six thousand women joined the three armed services during the second world war. Many more joined the women's land army to replace male rural workers. Others worked in war industries. But the significant female contribution to the war effort has largely gone uncelebrated. Few of the benefits available to returned servicemen were offered to them.

The first world war had contributed to the wider role of women in society because for the first time they had been allowed to join the workforce in numbers and areas unheard-of before. But in most cases, this emancipation was temporary. With the armistice came the expectation that women would return to hearth and home. Single women worked in a limited range of jobs in the interwar period, with only some determined and outstanding women pioneering the professions and other traditional male areas. So the battle had to be fought all over again during the second world war.

Employers, unions and government clashed over plans to use women in the depleted work force as the war progressed. Unions wanted an equal pay award, to ensure that women would not be a source of cheap labour after the war in competition with more expensive male employees. Employers, however, wanted cheap labour. The end result was a series of anomalies, with women in some industries achieving equal pay while in others they received substantially less. Some unions actually voted to reject women workers.

After the war, women faced a new struggle. They came under enormous pressure to leave their jobs in favour of the returning men. Their primary role was once more to be wives and mothers, committed to rebuilding family life as the bulwark against the new threat of communism in the cold-war period. It would take decades of slow struggle before women gained equal pay and equal rights as employees, and before it was considered socially acceptable for married women, particularly mothers, to be members of the work force. Today there are still anomalies in the system, and though women are now present in all employment areas, they are significantly under-represented at the top. Disproportionately few women are business executives, university professors, judges or community leaders, although there are outstanding exceptions to this general rule. Women remain seriously under-represented in Australian parliaments. In federal parliament, a recent count revealed that there are 26 women members out of a total of 224, and the situation is not very different in the state parliaments. Nevertheless, the present picture is a vast improvement on earlier years, when women members were a curiosity. The first women members of federal parliament were only elected in 1943.

Certainly the churches did nothing to encourage the full use of female talents in Australian post-war society. Church leaders and church women's organizations were sure that woman's place was in the home. They offered no other model for Christian women, and resisted even mild attempts to include women in church government. In some denominations and in some parts of Australia the rearguard action was stronger than in others. The role for women in most churches remained limited to fetes and flowers in the immediate post-war period.

Towards a multicultural Australia

After the war, the secularization of Australian society accelerated. There was a variety of attempts to stem the tide. The 1950s saw the Methodist Church throw enormous energy into a "Mission to the Nation", led by the Rev. (now Sir) Alan Walker. Most denominations, and particularly evangelical Anglicans, were involved in the 1959 Billy Graham crusades. Like the Walker mission, the emphasis was largely on individual conversion and a "return" to a high level of personal morality, particularly sexual. The nation would be redeemed through converting the multitudes, not by redeeming political or economic systems. The introduction of large-scale stewardship programmes at the same time offered a means of solving the problem of finance which had dogged the Australian churches since their beginnings.

Mostly the Protestant churches tackled their problems in ways that were directed at white Anglo-Celtic Australian culture. But even as they did so, that society was changing beyond all recognition in front of their eyes. The post-war period was a time of unprecedented boom in assisted migration to Australia, with more than four million people from 120 countries coming here between 1945 and 1989.

The Japanese threat had caused real concern that the Australian population — 7.4 million at the end of the second world war — was too small to defend adequately such a vast continent. A larger population was also necessary for full development of the Australian economy. Large-scale immigration was the only means to increase the population rapidly. The preference was of course for British migrants first and foremost and, with the white Australia policy still in force, any migration had to be European.

So began the era of the "ten pound poms". An assisted immigration scheme, which cost the British migrants no more than ten pounds each, was established between Britain and Australia, and resulted in large-scale British migration to this country. The British retained priority in immigration numbers until the assisted scheme ended during the 1970s. They also had special privileges in citizenship matters until that time. It has been estimated that, despite the presence of migrants from so many other ethnic groups in Australia, the British stream in the total population will still be about 70 percent at the end of this century.

Large numbers of migrants also came from eastern and southern Europe, in particular from Italy and Greece. The Italian and Greek elements in modern Australia have been significant and readily identifiable over the past few decades, and have influenced Australian society profoundly. The end of the white Australia policy in the 1970s, under the Whitlam Labor government, opened the door to numbers of migrants and

Sign in a Melbourne shop window testifies to cultural diversity... and a sense of humour (Barbara Matheson).

refugees from Asia and the Middle East, bringing inevitable changes to the Australian way of life. The change of policy from that of assimilation to integration at the same time has encouraged ethnic groups to retain and celebrate their cultural identity with all its richness and diversity. Under the assimilation policy, migrants were expected to abandon their old culture and adapt themselves to the British norms of their new home. The overall aim was the maintenance of the homogeneity of the society, but with such a large influx of people, it was never an attainable ideal.

So post-war Australian society is immeasurably richer than at any time in its history of European settlement. The last few decades have seen an explosion of artistic, intellectual and cultural energy in a great variety of forms, many of which are world-class. Gone is the dull, safe, sameness of the days when the performing arts and other cultural expressions were infrequent, second-rate or imported from overseas. Life-style, at least in the major cities, is international and cosmopolitan, though stamped with the influences of climate and the Australian preference for outdoor living.

Perhaps this is most noticeable in the enormous changes that have affected the diet of Australians. A generation ago, ordinary families ate plain food with an emphasis on beef and mutton, washed down with tea or beer. Coffee and wine were luxuries only enjoyed by the "society" class. Today inexpensive quality Australian wines are consumed regularly in the home, coffee is a favourite beverage, and foods once considered exotic — pastas, Mexican, Asian and Greek staple foods — are common menu items. A huge variety of ethnic restaurants continues to educate the Australian palate.

There lingers yet, however, an undercurrent of antipathy to migrants, particularly those from Asia. They are subjected more to subtle discrimination than outright attack, although anti-discrimination laws endeavour to protect their rights.

Vietnam

Australia's involvement in the wars of the twentieth century had caused limited opposition from some church people, mainly over specific areas such as conscription. But on the whole church leaders had not only supported war efforts but even blessed them. Not so, however, when, in 1964, the Menzies Liberal government introduced conscription to enable Australia to participate in the Vietnam war. Many Australians were opposed to the war, and not always on religious grounds. It was not so much an issue of pacifism, but rather of objection to Australia's involvement in this particular war, which had little other logic than support of America. So those in the churches who opposed the war and in particular, conscription, were not alone in the Australian community.

There was a high level of concerted action by church leaders and members alike, across the main denominations, opposing the war. Nine Anglican bishops wrote to the prime minister in March 1965 calling on the government to initiate a peaceful settlement. Alan Walker, of "Mission to the Nation" fame, set up a Canberra Vigil Committee to co-ordinate ecumenical war protests. A "Vigil for Peace" drew many clergy to Parliament House, Canberra, which was only the beginning of long-term anti-war action by church people across the country. The Australian Council of Churches called for a change in the law on conscientious objection, to allow objection to military service in a particular war, and was supported by a large number of Roman Catholic bishops.

The war protests, however, caused substantial internal conflicts for the churches. Radical young clergy found themselves in open dispute with their leaders, and conservatives targeted the anti-war movement for their main attack against liberalizing tendencies in the churches, particularly in the wake of Vatican II. Some commentators believe that the opposition to the Vietnam war, and the controversy and division it caused, were at least partly responsible for the accelerating withdrawal of the churches from their engagement at the centre of Australian life and politics.

In other ways, however, some members of the churches earned credibility with non-Christians across the whole area of secular activism. The churches continue to play a significant part in the modern peace movement, which is no longer as controversial as it was. It has become quite respectable these days, with archbishops and other leaders taking a prominent part in it. The churches' influence has ensured that Australia's main public peace commemoration is held on Palm Sunday.

Australian involvement in Vietnam, and conscription, came swiftly to an end with the coming to power of the Whitlam Labor government in 1972. Though its time in office was brief and controversial, its memorable election slogan, "It's time", signalled a deep restlessness in the Australian community for a break from the tired sameness of the previous long-reigning conservative regime, and the kind of society it symbolized. Though the Whitlam government was the first overtly secular Australian government, it was nevertheless welcomed by radical church people. It moved quickly to introduce some of the overdue items on their social justice shopping list, such as women's rights, Aboriginal land rights, and a more enlightened immigration policy, including the final dismantling of the white Australia policy.

Church and politics
The communist domination of the trade union movement began to cause real concern among prominent Roman Catholics during and after the second world war. Both the unions and the Catholics were traditionally powerful in the Australian Labor movement, so the growth of the power of the communists, nothing less than the anti-Christ to many Catholics, could only spell deep trouble for the Labor Party. Future problems loomed with the development of the "Movement", an anti-Communist Catholic organization which had its origins in Melbourne. Gaining the support of the Catholic bishops, it became an important national body after the second world war. Catholic interests coincided with those of the Labor Party's right wing, and so the scene was set for a powerful counter attack on communism.

The struggle to dethrone the communists in the unions spilt over into the Labor Party, where a fierce factional struggle eventually led to a split in the Labor Party itself. By 1957, a right-wing, Catholic-dominated national Democratic Labor Party was the result. For decades, it split the Labor vote, thus effectively keeping Labor out of power for long periods of time. For all its high-minded rhetoric of saving Australia from the communists and union domination, its ultimate achievement was to shore up the power of the conservative Liberal-Country Party governments, both at state and federal levels. Gough

Whitlam reshaped the Labor Party for victory at last in 1972 by appealing to the new suburban middle classes of the time, and the intelligentsia, the people most disaffected by the old-style Liberal regime and Australia's involvement in the Vietnam war. It was a new-style, pluralist Labor Party which came to power in the seventies and again in the eighties, pitted against an opposition that was increasingly less committed to white Protestant moralistic ideals. The days of the sectarian divide in Australian politics were finally over.

Union at last

Though earlier attempts to unite the Presbyterian, Methodist and Congregational churches had failed, the question was reopened during the second world war. The first new attempt failed, again because of Presbyterian dissent, in 1951. However, fresh initiatives just a few years later brought real hope. A Joint Commission on Church Union was formed in 1957, which produced a proposed basis of union in 1963. This was immediately controversial, because it proposed that the new church should include bishops, though with limited powers. Although there was substantial agreement on the union proposals from Congregationalists and Methodists, there was enough dissent from Presbyterian state assemblies and presbyteries to counsel caution. So negotiations continued, culminating in a revised basis of union published in 1971.

The following year Presbyterian communicants were asked to vote on the matter of union, but the wording of the questions created widespread confusion. So a second round of voting was necessary in 1973. Seventy-one percent of communicants voted to join the proposed new union. The differences between the states were interesting, further emphasizing the regional differences affecting all Australia's mainstream churches. In Victoria, always the most liberal and progressive state when it comes to the nature of its religious denominations, the vote for union was the highest, with only 24 percent of congregations voting to remain Presbyterian. That figure is especially significant when it is remembered that Presbyterianism was at its strongest in Victoria. In New South Wales however, 54 percent of the congregations voted to stay out of union, followed by Queensland with 46 percent.

It was now clear that the union of the three churches would mean that a continuing Presbyterian church would exist alongside it. After a bitter debate in the general assembly of Australia, held in May 1974, the necessary two-thirds mandate for union to proceed was achieved. Sadly, the matter then went to the civil courts, as continuing Presbyterians sought a legal ruling that the general assembly did not have the right to commit the church to union. The matter went as far as the high court of Australia, but the assembly's action was consistently upheld. The Uniting Church in Australia finally came into being on 22 June 1977.

A controversial beginning

The split in the Presbyterian Church was sad and unpleasant. Court cases ensued over the division of property, particularly in regard to some church schools. For some years after union, they remained contentious issues. These were not the only contentious issues, however. From the new church's beginnings, it has found itself embroiled in a number of controversies. In particular, its highly developed concern for social justice has kept its name in the media over issues such as Aboriginal rights, apartheid, nuclear energy, mining, and prison reform.

This record of public confrontation has not won the Uniting Church friends in high places. The Australian Protestant tradi-

A meeting of the Uniting Church's Uniting Aboriginal and Islander Christian Congress (New Times).

tion allows the churches a voice on moral and personal issues, but is often affronted when they attempt to influence the political or economic arenas. Religion is seen as a matter of private, individual piety. For this reason, it has not only been politicians and mining magnates who have been irritated by the Uniting Church's stand on many issues. Numbers of its own clergy and lay members have also been annoyed by statements that appear to have been issued in their name. "Who speaks for the Uniting Church?" is an ongoing question which has not yet been answered to the satisfaction of all.

The Uniting Church has not yet ironed out all the problems which must inevitably confront the marriage of three different traditions. It does not yet have a firm sense of identity; some of its members still feel themselves to be Presbyterian or Methodist or Congregationalist at heart. That is, however, a problem that will disappear within a generation or two. More seriously, in keeping with other Protestant churches, it is facing declining membership. Its congregations are statistically older than those of most other churches, and are certainly older than the general population.

Nevertheless, it is perhaps the most exciting Christian venture in Australia's history, an authentically indigenous church that transcends its past in the old world. It provides a vision of church unity which should inspire the other denominations. In its relatively short period of existence, it has achieved a remarkable degree of stability and cohesion. Its recent worship resource book, "Uniting in Worship", is quickly establishing itself as a contemporary work of outstanding liturgical excellence. And if the Uniting Church's actions have not always been popular, they have at least shown the wider community and the other churches that there is a positive place for an independent Christian voice in this country.

Goodbye to old England

The Uniting Church's very existence is an important symbol of a subtle psychological shift in Australian self-understanding. Despite federation, Gallipoli, and the American military connection, most Australians still saw themselves as part of the British empire as recently as two decades ago. Not many still called Britain "home", but nevertheless they were content that

Britain's national anthem, "God Save the Queen", was also Australia's national anthem. Governors-general, if no longer state governors, were, more often than not, sent out from Britain, as were some Anglican bishops. Final legal challenges could be sent to the British Privy Council. Any who questioned this situation, particularly the role of the British monarchy, were dismissed as ratbags or communists.

But gradually, imperceptibly, Australians had been changing. The Whitlam Labor government, coming to power in 1972, sensed a new day dawning and hastened its arrival. The dismissal of that government by the governor-general in 1975 in highly controversial circumstances had far-reaching effects. While it did not turn Australia into a republic, it aired the many issues of identity and self-determination that had been waiting in the wings for a long time. The later Hawke Labor government carried further what the Whitlam government began.

In the last decade of the twentieth century, the apron strings of Mother England are gone for good. The British monarch reigns over the Great South Land, but only in her capacity as Queen of Australia. Her titles here differ slightly from those she is accorded in Britain; in Australia she is not "Defender of the Faith", a symbolic reminder that there is no established religion in this country. The national anthem is now "Advance Australia Fair", a patriotic song written late last century. Green and gold, rather than the old "red, white and blue", are now Australia's national colours.

But the flag remains that adopted at the time of federation, after a competition which attracted 30,000 entries. Red, white and blue, the small Union Jack in its corner a reminder of the historic link with Britain, its truly distinctive feature is the Southern Cross, the star formation that is a prominent feature of the night sky in this hemisphere. It is a deliberate reminder of the flag flown at the Eureka Stockade. The flag, then, is a combination of British heritage and Australian independence.

A recent attempt to change the flag unleashed a strange and largely unexpected conservative reaction. "Keep this our flag forever" was emblazoned on bumper bars across the country, as Australians from many walks of life demonstrated a strong attachment to this national symbol. Too many Australians fought and died under the flag for it to be easily abandoned. Its echoes of an imperial past are just that, merely echoes. Australians are clear that the flag is, first and foremost, Australian. The colonial cringe is dead and buried, and a truly independent Australia is now mature enough to honour its past rather than submit slavishly to it or toss it out indiscriminately.

4. Conclusion: Land of the Spirit?

In the 1990s, Australia is a nation that is changing fast. The same sociological factors that are affecting most Western nations are at work here. Women now account for more than half the paid work force, and outnumber men in full-time tertiary education. They are found in almost every job and career, and many now run their own businesses. The "baby boomers", the post-war generation now approaching or negotiating middle age, are recognized by sociologists as a distinctive group fashioned by post-war prosperity and the television age. Some claim they are characterized by an unheard-of level of selfishness, and therefore easy prey in a consumer society. They represent a special challenge to churches still dominated by pre-1950s cultural expectations.

The population is ageing as life expectancy lengthens, and fewer babies are born. Men and women are marrying later, and 25 percent of women giving birth for the first time are now over thirty. *De facto* relationships are at an all-time high, 18 percent of children are born out of wedlock, and more than a third of marriages end in divorce. Only 36 percent of Australians actually live in a conventional nuclear family. Less traditional households are widely accepted, with divorcees, unmarried couples and single parents no longer stigmatized.

For the churches, these changes in public perceptions of personal morality have serious implications that few have properly confronted. While fundamentalist bodies and occasionally the mainstream churches castigate what they interpret as moral degeneracy, the churches are generally inclined to pretend it is not happening. The fact that respectable married people, traditional families and the widowed are in the pews, while divorcees, single mothers and *de facto* couples stay away, enables the pretence to continue.

Rites of passage

The churches are most affected by the societal changes around them when it comes to their ancient role as guardians of the rites of passage, and significant shifts have occurred there. Historically, civil marriages have not been popular in Australia. But in the decade of the seventies, the number of civil marriages sky-rocketted from one-tenth to more than one-third. This was mainly because civil marriage itself became a far more attractive option under new government regulations introduced during that time.

Civil marriages are no longer restricted to a registry office, within office hours, performed by a public servant. Today, licensed celebrants offer a variety of ceremonies in virtually any setting and at any time chosen by the bridal couple. The new breed of civil celebrants sometimes offers religionless naming and funeral ceremonies as well.

Comprehensive statistics of baptisms, confirmations and other indicators of formal church membership are not readily available across Australia, but all the signs suggest that the level of such admissions has fallen over the past decade or so. Fewer infants are being brought for baptism, and the number of teenage confirmations has declined drastically. This last, however, is as much a reflection of changing views of confirmation as it is of declining interest in the church among young people.

But despite the availability of secular funerals most funeral ceremonies, even when they are held in funeral parlours, still acknowledge a religious dimension. The vast majority of Australians still prefer the administration of funeral rites to be in the hands of the clergy.

Though no longer as universal as once they were, the Christian rites of passage still remain one of the few points of contact most Australians have with formal religion. Since the 1960s, church attendance has been declining in Australia at a rate that has been frightening. Though it has levelled off recently, the churches cannot afford any complacency. Attendances at the main Protestant denominations in the 1980s were half what they had been twenty-five years earlier. At the same time, 25 percent of the Australian population, according to the census figures, did not claim any religious affiliation. Half of those refused to state their position, but another 12 percent stated that they had "no religion". This is a dramatic increase on the 0.4 percent of the population who stated "no religion" a quarter of a century ago. This may represent nothing more than a greater degree of honesty, particularly amongst those nominal Christians who would once have called themselves "C of E" (Church of England/ Anglican). The number of Anglican adherents claimed in census figures has dropped by roughly the same numbers now claiming "no religion", in the same period of time.

Church-going

Surveys reveal that only about one-fifth of Australians claim to attend church each Sunday. One quarter say they are there at least once a month. These figures, however, may well be optimistic. Actual headcounts suggest that the true number of people attending church may well be somewhat lower. More than half Australians surveyed claim they have not attended a service of worship for more than a year.

The attendance figures vary considerably between denominations. Though Anglicans account for 24 percent of the population, according to census figures, only 10 percent of them attend church each week. Fifteen percent of the 11 percent of the population claiming to belong to the Uniting or Presbyterian Churches are regular attenders. Roman Catholics, who now account for 26 percent of Australians, for the first time edging ahead of the Anglicans, have a weekly attendance figure of almost 40 percent, a decline on previous generations.

Church-goers, however, do not represent a true sample of the wider population. In the main Protestant denominations, they tend to be more highly educated, and belong to higher socio-

Open-air Anglican Easter church service (World-wide Photos).

economic groups, than average. They also tend to be Australian-born; in other words, drawn primarily from the British stream in Australian society. On average, they are also older than the general population. Women are far more regular in church attendance than men, and both men and women in the 18-30 age-range are largely absent from the churches. On the other hand, the profile of Roman Catholic congregations is more truly representative of the wider population, including a wider cross-section of educational and working backgrounds as well as better representation of migrant communities.

While the mainline churches have declined, the Pentecostal churches have experienced a boom. They are enjoying strong growth, in particular attracting those people least attracted to the traditional churches. Their congregations are significantly younger than those of other churches, and many commentators believe that they have picked up the generation lost by the others. Their congregations, and their clergy, are also significantly less well-educated than those of their counterparts. They tend to attract tradespeople rather than graduates, and so appeal to a socio-economic group previously alienated from institutional Protestant Christianity.

One interesting statistic indicates that the age-old concern of the church for the wider community is still exemplified by contemporary Australian congregations. Regular church-goers still demonstrate a much higher commitment to community work of all kinds than the general population. Their involvement in charity/welfare, youth work and human rights groups is three times as high, while their work for general community groups is at least double. Another survey among Anglicans suggests that racist attitudes are less likely to be found among church-goers than among the general population.

Another statistic suggests that the churches and their related bodies may yet have the potential to convey the Christian message to a far greater clientele than that represented by their worshippers. One-third of Australian secondary school students now attend private schools, a significant rise over the past twenty years. Almost all private schools in Australia, from elite grammar schools to low-fee community colleges, have some connection with Christian denominations, either directly or indirectly. Though parents choose these schools on educational grounds, most readily accept the religious affiliation they represent. These schools then, through their worship services and religious education programmes, have a golden opportunity to create at least a sympathy for institutional religion in the wider community in a way denied to the parish churches.

Certainly that has been the pattern on a much smaller scale in the past. Leading church-related schools have educated the nation's elite for well over a century. Recent surveys indicate that their influence is still powerful. For example, former students of Victoria's five top schools — two Anglican, one Catholic, one Presbyterian and one Uniting Church — still dominate the top echelons of the worlds of business, law, medicine, academe and diplomacy. Many of them retain at least a nominal commitment to the church and respect for its place in society.

These schools have also in the past provided the Protestant churches with generations of lay people who believed it to be their duty to offer their talents and support at many levels of church government. Some schools also produced a particularly high number of clergy as well.

Secular spirituality

But neither the census figures nor the statistics on church-going reveal the total story about contemporary religion in Australia in the last decade of the twentieth century. There is in fact a religious dimension which has only tenuous links with institutional religion. Indeed, it is a dimension that seems to be thriving despite the churches. Though mainstream Protestantism is in decline and Roman Catholicism has ceased to command unswerving loyalty, public interest in religious issues and spirituality is strong.

Recent surveys reveal that 58 percent of Australians claim to be religious persons, and regard God as being important in their lives. Only 4.5 percent of the population call themselves atheists. Two-thirds of Australians say that they pray, meditate or contemplate at least occasionally, and nearly 86 percent still want to identify with a particular denomination or religious group.

These findings show that Australia's self-image as a secular society needs to be carefully evaluated. Commentators interpret

Some Comments about What it Means to be a Christian in Australia Today

"It means being misunderstood. People think we are better than they are because we attend church" — Churches of Christ minister, Melbourne.

"Christian churches have a wowser image. They have tended to react against social and justice issues instead of setting the agenda themselves" — Catholic layman, Melbourne.

"Being a Christian is a hell of a lot of work. We have a responsibility for finding solutions to society's problems" — Catholic parish meeting group response, Melbourne.

"Being a Christian is getting more and more exciting. More and more people are coming to respect faith as they lose their trust in materialism" — Uniting Church woman, 40, Tasmania.

"It is frustrating and depressing being a Christian in Australia today. The vast majority of the population seems to be spiritually dead" — Anglican man, 36, Tasmania.

"The Christian Church can no longer claim to have the strong influence over people's lives that it once enjoyed" — Churchgoer, Tasmania.

"To be a Christian in Australia today means to belong to a 'fellowship of the concerned'" — Uniting Church woman, 67, South Australia.

"I can no longer participate in the brokenness of the body of Christ; it is time to renounce the divisions and separation of the body of Christ. It is not enough merely to pray for unity" — Christian man, formerly Uniting Church, NSW.

"I pray and hope the church will open its arms to those who need it most; most of the people who land in prison have never been really and wisely loved" — Anglican woman, 73, South Australia.

"Archaic ecclesiastical dress and pomp and ceremony has no appeal to those outside our congregations" — Anglican man, Queensland.

"Being a Christian means to be like Christ" — Seventh Day Adventist woman, 82, Melbourne.

"Church allegiance is more respected in Australia now than it was ten or twenty years ago. The church's greatest problem today is the undue time spent on maintaining the structure, both buildings and hierarchy" — Uniting Church woman, mid-60s, Tasmania.

"In Australian society, religion is taboo as a discussion subject in the work place. A Christian can work alongside another Christian without knowing it" — Uniting Church man, NSW.

"The significant religious tension is between Christian theists and secularists, and the old squabbles between Christians are anachronistic, wrong in principle and practice" — Bishop George Pell, Melbourne.

"Being a Christian can be tough at times when you are around your friends, but it can also be fun and worthwhile" — Anglican boy, 12, NSW.

"Because I'm a P.K. (Priest's Kid), other kids treat me different" — Greek Orthodox boy, 13, NSW.

"It is an enormous headache to be a Christian in Australia, but God makes it bearable" — Presbyterian boy, 15, NSW.

the seeming contradiction between church-going and personal spirituality differently. It does seem, however, that while institutional religion is not attractive to most Australians, and some even find it alienating, they are not godless as so many church leaders have feared. The religious dimension is important, and many Australians seek an active relationship with God, though not via the churches.

From the churches' perspective, however, this persistent and surprising spirituality in the wider population presents real problems. The downturn in church attendance over the past thirty years, particularly among young people, means that a whole generation has missed out on even the most basic Christian education. So numbers of Australians simply do not know the Christian story, let alone have any familiarity with Christian ritual, even the Lord's prayer.

If the churches are to make use of the strong community interest in religion, then they will have to do more than simply invite people to church. Traditional church worship is an alien experience to most Australians, and much that passes for modern worship is only marginally less so. If so many people find that they can gratify their need for religion outside the institution, then the institution has to work very hard to convince them otherwise. Evangelism is every bit as challenging — and as daunting — in Australia at this period of time as it is in any other part of the world.

Is Australia then any more secular than other comparable nations today? Some have pointed out that New Zealand society is just as secular by every indicator, including the level of church attendance, as Australia, and that despite a much less secular colonial past. There are no convicts in New Zealand's past, so it did not begin its Christian history in despair. There is no terrifying outback or vast, unimaginable distances to instil a sense of fatalism. Perhaps it is just that New Zealand has caught up with its next-door neighbour. Perhaps Australia's uniqueness in this regard lies in the historical power of its strident secularity, bred equally by its harsh beginnings and its harsh, overpowering terrain. It has created a people who keep their mysticism to themselves, and keep the churches at bay unless they can prove that they have something concrete to offer to a race that likes to see itself as essentially down-to-earth.

Transplanting the past

Historically, the churches' record in Australia is not good. For two hundred years, they have struggled to find their place in the great south land. They have made many mistakes, many of them quite unwittingly.

Aliens in an alien land, half a world away from home, they tried to re-create their homeland and all that made its memories so dear. So they built Gothic-style stone churches with tiny windows that closed out the view of the endless plains; planted yew trees in their churchyards; and celebrated Christmas as a mid-winter festival despite the scorching summer sun.

The Christianity they transplanted was nostalgic, evoking the certainties of the old world amid the uncertainties of the new. They sought to re-establish the old order, but mostly failed, defeated by the vast distances and determined secularity of the new country. Tragically, in the process, they succeeded in entrenching the ancient sectarian feuds that had bedevilled religion in Britain for centuries.

These feuds are, thankfully, mostly a thing of the past. There will always be small pockets of bitterness against one or another of the mainstream denominations, but on the whole, relationships between Protestants and Roman Catholics are now deep and genuine. There is a high level of co-operation among the churches, so much so that the Australian Council of Churches and the Australian Catholic Bishops' Conference have formed a working party to investigate the possibility of a new, enlarged national body that will include both Protestant and Catholic churches.

If the scandal of division has been largely overcome, the legacy of the puritan Protestant past still insulates numbers of Australians from the joy of Christianity. The "wowser" response to the excesses of frontier life meant that Christian commitment became quickly equated with an obsessional concern with personal behaviour. Only individual salvation, demonstrated through a rigid conformity to a narrow code of public conduct, could redeem the nation generally and the working classes specially, the wowsers insisted. This harsh puritanical streak has done great harm to the public perception of institutional religion in Australia. In the last decade of the twentieth century, long after the "golden age" of the wowsers, it remains a

Aborigines in a bush camp outside the Papunya reserve, Central Australia (Australian Council of Churches).

persistent legacy. The general public still expects religious people, and clergy in particular, to be somewhat less than red-blooded. Some ministers, anxious to assure their followers of their exemplary behaviour, fulfill these expectations. It is a legacy that has to be overcome before the Christian churches can attract real community following.

The historical obsession with individual salvation, exemplified not only by the wowser tradition but by the tradition of evangelistic missions as well, has left Australian Christians with a very limited sense of corporate identity. They rarely see themselves as a "people of God", but rather as, first and foremost, individual believers. There are notable exceptions, where congregations do offer alternative communities. But generally Christians have little sense of true community to offer a generation that misses the communities that flourished before rapid rural decline and the growth of dormitory suburbs destroyed them.

An Australian theology?

There is still only a very limited indigenous theology. This is partly because the churches are still governed in some measure by their past. Protestant church structures, processes and liturgies retain their British flavour. Even where modern local alternatives have been developed, they have often been adopted somewhat apologetically. The Anglican Church's *An Australian Prayer Book* (1978) and the Uniting Church's *Uniting in Worship* (1988) are good examples of this tendency. Both are exciting and valuable liturgical resources of international standard.

But though the Anglican book has been overwhelmingly accepted by congregations across the country, the church's hierarchy, anxious not to displease a tiny minority of opponents of the book, continues to pay lip-service to its sixteenth-century English forerunner. More than a decade after its publication, the *Australian Prayer Book* still waits for the unqualified affirmation it deserves. Similarly, the virtues of *Uniting in Worship* deserve to be trumpeted from the rooftops.

The development of a genuine Australian theology has been severely hampered by the continuing immigrant mentality of the Australian churches. The wider culture has abandoned the colonial cringe and now exults in the uniqueness of the wide brown land. Australians are ready for an authentic spiritual interpretation of their national experience in all its dimensions. But by and large the churches are confused about how to break the last tenuous threads of the umbilical cord. Because in so many ways they stand apart from society, some attempts to Australianize the Christian faith have been monumental flops. Translating Bible stories into Aussie slang or writing psalms and hymns dependent on self-consciously Australian imagery of gum trees and kangaroos have rarely worked. Attempts to recreate God and Jesus in "ocker" terms have similarly been failures.

Abandoning gimmicks, a small but significant number of Australian theologians has preferred to explore the possibility of pursuing great universal themes from the distinctive perspective of the Australian context. Some of Australia's leading literary and creative artists, though most of them are not professing Christians, have already pioneered the way. Self-professed atheist novelist Patrick White is an obvious example, as is agnostic historian Manning Clark, whose prolific writings are haunted by his vicarage childhood. The great danger, as some theologians have recognized, lies in the determination of just what that Australian context is anyway. Is it primarily the Australian legend, or the Australian reality? Does Australian theologizing begin with the laconic lone bushman, the failed male hero of Eureka and Gallipoli, or with the suburban women and men of modern, technocratic, multicultural Australia? Or does indigenous theology begin and end with the major ideological issues of this place and time, and thus risk neglecting the everyday pettiness and frustratingly limited horizons that are the lot of ordinary people?

The issues

The big ideological issues facing the churches cannot, however, be ignored. Some of those challenging Australian Christians today are universal concerns. For instance, the role of women is confronting many churches around the world. The World Council of Churches' Ecumenical Decade of Churches in Solidarity with Women indicates the extent of the concern. But there are nevertheless important Australian perspectives on this question. Other issues are fundamentally local, such as concern for Aborigines and the multicultural direction of contemporary Australian society. Other local issues are less dramatic, but very real. In still other areas, such as bio-ethics, the pioneering work of Australian medicine is forcing Australian theologians to pioneer areas that will eventually be of wide international interest.

1. The Aborigines

For 200 years, white Australians tended to put the questions regarding the Aborigines on the back burner. At times, particularly over the past twenty years, individual events have prompted a raising of concern. The growing urgency of the issue of land rights and the increasing contribution of Aborigines themselves to the various debates, raised consciousness at many levels. Increasingly churches argued their case, particularly over the land question. But in 1988, the year in which

Aboriginal nativity painting (Keith Cole).

Australia celebrated the bicentenary of white settlement, the issue came to a head as never before.

Suddenly Australians from all walks of life found themselves confronted with the fact that white settlement was also white invasion; that while Europeans had been here for 200 years, Aboriginal history went back at least 40,000 years. Uneasy controversy erupted, as Aboriginal activists and their white supporters — some of whom were also Christian leaders — gently brought the facts home. There were some displays of anger, but the primary emotion was that of grief. There were poignant scenes as Aborigines cast mourning wreaths on the oceans that had brought the white conquerors who devastated their race.

As white Australians tried to deal with their discomforting discovery, theologians recognized that this pain seared the Australian soul. Deep in the national psyche lay a powerful guilt over the treatment of Aborigines. Successfully repressed for generations, it had now emerged to haunt the celebration of a nation. The year-long party was tinged with sorrow. Until the situation is redressed, the pain will not be healed.

It is not simply the past that must be redeemed, but the present as well. Aborigines are still denied many of the benefits of life in the "lucky country". The statistics tell the story. The life expectancy of Aborigines is twenty years less than for white people, while child mortality is three times higher than the national average. Aboriginal mothers are eight times more likely to die in childbirth than white mothers. The rates of some diseases are much higher among Aboriginal people, with the levels of the eye disease trachoma a special tragedy. More than a third of Aboriginal children, compared with 1.6 percent of non-Aboriginal children, suffer from it.

Aborigines suffer much higher unemployment rates than whites, and on average earn only half the income of other Australians. They are sixteen times more likely to be imprisoned. The recent epidemic of Aboriginal deaths in custody, the subject of a high-level inquiry, is the symptom of the continuing injustice and misunderstanding that marks relationships between Aboriginal and non-Aboriginal Australians.

Tackling these appalling statistics requires more than a massive injection of funds and remedial measures, necessary as they are. Aborigines must be enabled to claim back the ancient dignity of their race, and wear it with pride. To do that, they must be given back their land, not only because it would allow independent economic development, but also because the land itself is central to Aboriginal life and spirituality. This is a controversial issue, and one that will not easily be resolved. In particular, mining and pastoral interests are fiercely opposed to attempts to give significant holdings of traditional lands into Aboriginal ownership. Nevertheless, large transfers of land have taken place, and in some parts of outback Australia Aborigines once more control a portion at least of their tribal territories.

Some governments and some political parties have tackled the land rights question better than others, but there have been signs of a weakening of commitment in recent years. The federal Labor government has backed away from earlier commitments to land rights and the concept of a treaty with

Australia's first Aborigine-owned commercial television station, the Central Australian Aboriginal Media Association (CAAMA), broadcasts over a vast central area to a 40 percent Aboriginal audience (Bill Payne/Promotion Australia).

Aborigines. The mainline Christian churches have urged a just resolution as central to real reconciliation between black and white Australians. Pope John Paul II, visiting Alice Springs in central Australia in 1986, lent his support to land rights.

Covenant: The Uniting Church, always at the forefront of justice issues, is pioneering the concept of a covenant between the church's Aboriginal and non-Aboriginal members. Representatives of the church's national assembly and of the Uniting Aboriginal and Islander Christian Congress are working together on the covenant process. The Congress, formed in 1985, gives a distinctive voice to Aboriginal people, and a structure where decision-making is not dominated by European models. Aboriginal and Islander ministries and congregations are united under its care. Outstanding Aboriginal lay and ordained leaders have merged in the Uniting Church.

The Anglican Church has an Aboriginal bishop and a Torres Strait Islander bishop, and increasing numbers of Aboriginal clergy. Clergy and lay people of the Anglican and Uniting Churches are trained together at Nungalinya College, Darwin, and with Catholics as well, through Wontulp-Bi-Buya which provides ecumenical theological education by extension from its base in Townsville, North Queensland.

Sadly, the Roman Catholic Church has no serving Aboriginal priests, the celibacy law being completely foreign to traditional culture. But there is an Aboriginal and Islander Catholic Council, and a high level of commitment to Aboriginal issues at many levels. The outstanding leadership of Jesuit priest Frank Brennan, advisor on Aboriginal issues to the Australian Catholic bishops, is widely recognized.

The Australian Council of Churches has formed an Aboriginal and Islander Commission, designed to be a "real force for Aboriginal and Islander people in religious, social, and political life" in Australia. It is seen as an important step towards reconciliation of the races.

Christianity has been flourishing among Aboriginal people in Northern Australia in what amounts to an extraordinary spiritual revival over the past fifteen years. Aboriginal people have assumed full responsibility for their congregations, and have a dynamic sense of mission towards their own people. In an exciting process of inculturation, they are successfully integrating the

Christian gospel into Aboriginal culture and traditional belief systems. So the worship of Aboriginal communities has a refreshing internal integrity, and sits easily to a wide spectrum of Christian tradition. Ecumenism comes naturally to Aborigines.

Aboriginal theologians are proclaiming a God who has lived with them throughout their history, who gave them the Dreaming, and spoke to them through it. Aboriginal artists are conveying Christian truths through traditional media and traditional art forms. And together they are offering their insights and the deep spirituality of their race as a generous gift towards the healing of the materialism and cynicism of so many white Australians.

2. The place of women

Australia's two largest churches still lag behind the wider community in their attitude to women. While both the Roman Catholic and Anglican Churches protest that they hold women to be fully equal to men, the fact remains that women are barred, on grounds of gender alone, from full participation in the ordained ministry in those churches. Thus the churches which nominally represent 50 percent of Australians, and some two-thirds of Australian Christians, would fail to qualify as employers under the nation's equal opportunity legislation. That legislation, however, specifically exempts religious bodies.

The Australian Roman Catholic Church does not have the authority to change the local situation. Nevertheless, there is growing grassroots support for an enhanced role for women at all levels. The women's religious orders are particularly important in this area, and lay women are being encouraged to make their opinions known through a nation-wide organization, Women and the Australian Church (WATAC). The numbers of women students in Catholic theological colleges around Australia is steadily increasing.

The Anglican Church has agonized over the question of women priests for two decades, and there is now wide support across the country for women's ordination. However, the stringent requirements of the church's national constitution, which insist on high voting majorities on matters of church law, have seen the move fail a number of times. In 1989, there were ninety women deacons in Australia, most of whom wish to be ordained to the priesthood.

The other Protestant denominations have pioneered women's ministry in Australia. The first Congregational minister was ordained as early as 1927 in Adelaide. The Methodist Church followed suit in 1969, followed by the Presbyterians in 1974. There have been ordained women ministers in the Baptist Church and Churches of Christ since 1973 and 1978 respectively, though their numbers remain small. Today the Uniting Church has 138 women clergy.

There is intense public interest in the question of women's ordination, particularly as the Anglican Church's struggle continues to capture headlines. Many people in the wider community are genuinely mystified at church reluctance to welcome women into the ministry, and some believe that the churches' credibility is at stake while this issue remains unresolved.

3. The challenge of multiculturalism

The huge influx of migrants since the second world war has changed the face of Australian society in many ways. There is the obvious change in life-style, touched on earlier. There are also more subtle changes, such as a growing respect for the place of religion in areas once deemed to be secular. For instance, educational authorities are increasingly recognizing that religion is often integral to ethnic identity, and therefore must be taken seriously if multiculturalism is to be taken seriously. Surveys have revealed that migrants from Southern and Eastern Europe, as well as from Asia, rate their religious identity very highly. This means that there is now a greater sympathy for the teaching of religious studies in state school systems, if for no other reason than to increase community understanding of minority groups and their concerns.

In statistical terms, however, Australia is not truly a multi-faith nation. Together, those who call themselves Christian (73 percent of the population) and those who do not acknowledge any religious belief (24.6 percent) account for 97.6 percent of Australians. Other religions have grown by enormous percentage points in recent years, but the overall numbers still remain small. Altogether, they accounted for 2 percent of the population at the 1986 census.

The largest of these religions, Islam (0.7 percent), has trebled since 1971 through migration. Most Muslim migrants have settled in Sydney. Buddhists (0.5 percent) have a more complex background in Australia. Asian migrants, particularly from Vietnam, have boosted the Buddhist following, but there is also a long tradition of adherence by converts from Christianity. There is an interest in Buddhist teachings and meditational practices among the wider community, though these people would not classify themselves as Buddhists. All three major traditions of Buddhism are represented in Australia.

Orthodox churches: In religious terms, multicultural diversity has far greater expression in the development or growth of a variety of Christian churches, and of diversity within the mainstream churches. The large-scale migration from Greece has boosted the size and influence of the Greek Orthodox church in this country. The presence of the Orthodox church here dates back to before the turn of the century, but it was the post-war influx of Greek people which saw the rapid growth of the denomination. The Orthodox churches together now constitute the fifth largest denomination.

The Greek Orthodox Archdiocese of Australia is divided into five districts, with a total of more than 100 churches and clergy. There are community centres, social services, and afternoon schools which enable Greek language and culture, as well as religion, to be transmitted to the growing generation. Many of the students, however, keen to see themselves as real "Aussies", chafe under their parents' wish for them to be bicultural.

The other Orthodox churches in Australia include the Antiochian, Russian (Abroad), Serbian, Romanian, Bulgarian, Ukrainian and Macedonian. Other Eastern Christian churches are also represented in Australia, including the Armenian Apostolic Church, and the Holy Apostolic Catholic Assyrian Church of the East.

The Lutherans: The Lutheran Church is an older "ethnic" church in Australia. It owes its beginnings to waves of German immigration last century, particularly to areas around Adelaide in South Australia. Lutheran missions to the Aborigines have a particularly fine record, especially the work among the Aranda tribe in central Australia. Much of the history of Lutheranism in Australia is marked by complex groupings and disunity, but the factions all came together finally when the Lutheran Church of Australia was formed in 1966. Today Lutherans account for 1.3 percent of the population. Recently a joint working party has been established between the Lutheran Church and the Australian Council of Churches, aimed at creating a wider ecumenical body which they can join.

The challenge

The mainstream churches are trying to come to terms with the challenge of the changing cultural face of Australia. The Roman Catholic Church, once so powerfully Irish in its style and therefore suspicious of the rich varieties of Catholicism being brought to Australia by migrant worshippers, now celebrates that diversity. It is proud of the many ethnic groups which make up Catholic congregations.

The other churches, in varying degrees, are struggling to find their place in the new society. Unlike the Roman Catholic Church, the Protestant churches have not had their figures significantly boosted by post-war immigration. Those they have gained from the stream of British newcomers have fitted readily into the Australian churches. But most are aware that they have a responsibility to minister to the newcomers, particularly those

Greek, Vietnamese and a bit of English explain this Melbourne church's programme (Barbara Matheson).

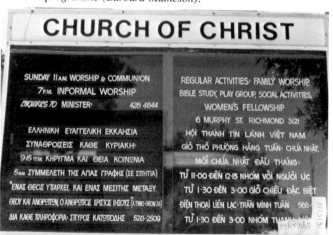

who have either no Christian background, or one that has no obvious home in this community.

There are some outstanding examples of work among Asians in particular by some local parishes. Often these were traditional Anglo-Celtic congregations in decline because of large-scale immigration into their areas. So the outreach to the newcomers has been a life-saver for the congregations concerned. The methods differ. Sometimes the congregational worship pattern has been adapted to make it more accessible to outsiders; in other places, separate worship services for people of one particular ethnic group are held.

In Melbourne in particular, where the racial and ethnic mix is greatest, the mainstream Anglican, Uniting, Baptist and Churches of Christ churches have all committed themselves to multicultural ministry in some shape or form. The big question facing all the churches as they find themselves ministering to people from different faith traditions is: do they seek primarily to convert the newcomers, or to respect their faith position while serving them in the name of Christ?

4. Bio-ethics

Australian scientists have been at the forefront of world developments in the field of bio-ethics. In particular, in vitro fertilization (IVF) procedures have developed rapidly, and now most states have programmes in place. They continue to be a source of controversy, as scientists, governments, feminist groups and others ask hard questions about what kind of "brave new world" is in the making. Some, particularly women's groups, fear that the costly, time-consuming and too often unsuccessful attempts to achieve pregnancies benefit the medical profession more often than childless women. But church social responsibilities committees are more concerned with the ethical issues involved in embryo research and surrogate parenting. Protestant churches mostly accept IVF (though sometimes uneasily) for married couples, but the Roman Catholic Church condemns it on the ground that it transgresses the natural law. The role of the churches in these ethical deliberations is recognized. All institutional ethics committees include at least one minister of religion, and sometimes two.

Church life in the 1990s

The Christian churches face many internal problems in the last decade of the twentieth century. The Roman Catholic Church, now the largest in Australia and with a relatively high rate of church attendance, is facing a major crisis in terms of its priesthood. Large archdioceses like Sydney and Melbourne are seeing only a handful of priests ordained each year at the most. The number of ordinands is at an all-time low. Increasingly full-time pastoral associates — often members of women's religious orders — are taking over work once restricted to clergy.

The Anglican Church is finding it more and more difficult to operate nationally. The cost of supporting a national profile and national programmes is rising disproportionately. The "tyranny of distance", which has dogged white Australian settlement from its beginnings, is primarily to blame. Other issues, such as the ordination of women, are also pushing the churches towards a greater sense of regional autonomy.

The growth of Pentecostal churches, and Evangelical and "New Right" fundamentalism, both secular and religious, have all had their impact on the churches. Attempts to engage with the world in the 1960s and 70s, particularly over political issues such as the Vietnam war, were traumatic in some instances. Recent research has shown that across all the denominations, contemporary clergy have become more introverted, seeing their role as God- and-church centred first and foremost. They are reluctant to venture into community issues.

Australian churches have been connected with the World Council of Churches since its inception in 1948. Three churches — the Anglican, Uniting and Churches of Christ — are direct members while others such as the Orthodox and Oriental churches are linked through their hierarchies overseas. Only two member churches of the Australian Council of Churches — the Salvation Army and the Society of Friends — are not members of the World Council.

Their involvement in the World Council of Churches has been influential on all these churches, giving a greater impact on everyday church life than most Australian Christians realize. Without this involvement, local ecumenical initiatives such as the creation of the Uniting Church, the development of co-operative theological education, industrial chaplaincy, and joint social justice statements, would not have developed as they have done.

With Australians increasingly realizing that they are a part of Asia rather than Europe, particularly in matters of trade, the churches' involvement in the Christian Conference of Asia is likely to have a growing impact. Australia has been a member of the Conference since its inception in 1957. It is significant that Australia's regional ecumenical activity is based in Asia rather than the Pacific. It was by mutual decision that Australia opted to join the Asian conference rather than the Pacific Conference of Churches, reflecting the political and economic realities of the whole region.

At the local level, the ecumenical movement is not as far advanced as it might be among Australian Christians. With some honourable exceptions, congregations of different denominations usually worship or work together only on special occasions. "Carols by candlelight", a simple outdoor Christmas service designed for non-church-goers, has become a popular ecumenical event in many localities. But such occasions are few and far between. There continues to be too much duplication of activities in areas where ecumenical co-operation would ensure a better use of available resources.

However, there is nevertheless a high level of goodwill between Christians of all denominations, and a sense of being engaged on a common task. At leadership level, there is often a greater degree of sharing and co-operation, with the "heads of churches", representing fourteen Christian bodies, coming together from time to time to make public statements on important issues.

Land of the Spirit?

Most church leaders are anxious to ensure that the Christian faith has a significant impact on Australian life. Few of them speak in terms of a "Christian Australia" any more, preferring a vision of a nation following general Christian values to a nation battened down under strict rules governing personal morality. Nevertheless, they would like to believe that the transformation of Australian society under the power of the gospel was a realistic goal for the future. But the failures of the past haunt them as they face the complexities of the present. How best can the Christian churches make their mark?

There are signs that the wider Australian community will listen seriously to the churches once certain conditions are met. In the land of the "fair go", where deeds speak louder than words, high-flown ideals are viewed with suspicion and authoritarianism is despised, the churches and their leaders have to demonstrate, first and foremost, that they care. Once they do, they gain real respect. So the Salvation Army is universally respected because its name is synonymous with practical welfare work. "Flynn of the Inland" is a legend because he not only recognized the desperate isolation of outback Australians, but did something about it.

David Penman, Anglican archbishop of Melbourne who died suddenly at the age of 53 in 1989, achieved an astonishingly high public following in a brief five years in office. In sport-mad Melbourne, his passion for football and cricket gave him an all-important image as a man of the people. But more than that, he came across as one who cared passionately about the concerns of ordinary people. Never frightened to tackle controversial issues, he directly engaged himself in local, national and international issues, drawing no distinction between sacred and secular. The media were always interested in his comments, and the general public listened attentively. His death saw a whole city plunged into mourning.

In secular Australia, the church need be on the sidelines only if that is where it wishes to be. If it respects and cares for those among whom it is set, it will be respected in return.

Is Australia the South Land of the Holy Spirit? Most Australians, in their inimitable way, would shy clear of such a flowery description. But like the Aborigines who have known this country as "land of the Spirit" since the time of the Dreaming, many white Australians today find spiritual value in the very terrain their ancestors found so terrifying. There are deep springs of spiritual values, too, underlying the so-called secular society. They are simply waiting to be baptized by a church generous enough to recognize that they are of God.

Suggested Reading

John Barrett, *That Better Country: the Religious Aspect of Life in Eastern Australia 1835-1850*, Melbourne University Press, Melbourne, 1966

Ian Breward, *Australia, "the Most Godless Place under Heaven"?*, Beacon Hill Books, 1988

J.D.Bollen, *Religion in Australian Society, an Historian's View*, The Leigh College Open Lectures, Winter Series, 1973

Edmund Campion, *Australian Catholics*, Viking, Melbourne, 1987

Miriam Dixson, *The Real Matilda: Woman and Identity in Australia 1788 to the Present*, Penguin, rev. ed., Melbourne, 1984

Andrew Dutney, *From Here to Where? Australian Christians Owning the Past — Embracing the Future*, Uniting Church Press, 1988

Frank Engel, *Australian Christians in Conflict and Unity*, Joint Board of Christian Education, Melbourne, 1984

Ian Gillman ed., *Many Faiths One Nation: a Guide to the Major Faiths and Denominations in Australia*, Collins, Sydney, 1988

Peter Kaldor, *Going to Church in Australia: Who Goes Where? Who Doesn't Care?*, Lancer Books, Sydney, 1987

Michael Hogan *The Sectarian Strand: Religion in Australian History*, Penguin, Melbourne, 1987

Robert Hughes, *The Fatal Shore*, Collins Harvill, London, 1987

Douglas Hynd, *Australian Christianity in Outline: a Statistical Analysis and Directory*, Lancer Books, Sydney, 1984

Peter Malone ed., *Discovering an Australian Theology*, St Paul Publications, Sydney, 1988

David Millikan, *The Sunburnt Soul, Christianity in Search of an Australian Identity*, Lancer Books, Sydney, 1981

Sally Morgan, *My Place,* Fremantle Arts Centre Press, 1987 (a moving account of one Aboriginal family's experience of death and resurrection)

William Tabbernee ed., *Initiation in Australian Churches*, Victorian Council of Churches, Melbourne, 1984; *Marriage in Australian Churches*, VCC, 1982; *Ministry in Australian Churches*, VCC-JBCE, 1987

Russell Ward, *The Australian Legend*, Oxford University Press, Melbourne, 1958

Bruce Wilson, *Can God Survive in Australia?*, Albatross, Sydney, 1983